ENGAGE WITH RAGE

SAMMY FRANCO

Also by Sammy Franco

War Machine II
1001 Street Fighting Secrets
Combat Pressure Points
Cane Fighting
Double End Bag Training
The Heavy Bag Bible
The Widow Maker Compendium
Invincible: Mental Toughness Techniques for Peak Performance
Unleash Hell: A Step-by-Step Guide to Devastating Widow Maker Combinations
Feral Fighting: Advanced Widow Maker Fighting Techniques
The Widow Maker Program: Extreme Self-Defense for Deadly Force Situations
Savage Street Fighting: Tactical Savagery as a Last Resort
Heavy Bag Combinations
Heavy Bag Training
The Complete Body Opponent Bag Book
Stand and Deliver: A Street Warrior's Guide to Tactical Combat Stances
Maximum Damage: Hidden Secrets Behind Brutal Fighting Combinations
First Strike: End a Fight in Ten Seconds or Less
The Bigger They Are, The Harder They Fall
Self-Defense Tips and Tricks
Kubotan Power: Quick & Simple Steps to Mastering the Kubotan Keychain
Gun Safety: For Home Defense and Concealed Carry
Out of the Cage: A Guide to Beating a Mixed Martial Artist on the Street
Warrior Wisdom: Inspiring Ideas from the World's Greatest Warriors
War Machine: How to Transform Yourself Into a Vicious Street Fighter
When Seconds Count: Self-Defense for the Real World
Killer Instinct: Unarmed Combat for Street Survival
Street Lethal: Unarmed Urban Combat

Engage With Rage
Copyright © 2024 by Sammy Franco
ISBN: 978-1-941845-83-7
Printed in the United States of America
Visit online at: ContemporaryFightingArts.com

All rights reserved. Except for use in a review, no portion of this book may be reproduced in any form without the express written permission of the author.

*For my mother, Barbara Franco,
a woman of great courage.*

ENGAGE WITH RAGE

Contents

About This Book   ix

Introduction   1
What is Contemporary Fighting Arts?

Chapter One   15
Fighting Ranges

Chapter Two   23
The Inside Position

Chapter Three   53
Anchoring the Aggressor

Chapter Four   67
Target Areas & Techniques

Chapter Five   111
Extreme Clinch Fighting

Chapter Six   143
Countering Attacks in the Clinch

Chapter Seven   179
Takedown Defenses

Chapter Eight   209
Clinch Conditioning

Glossary   217

Suggested Reading & Viewing   257

About Sammy Franco   261

"If I wish to engage, then the enemy, for all his high ramparts and deep moat, cannot avoid engagement; I attack that which he is obliged to rescue."

– Sun Tzu

Disclaimer

The author, publisher, and distributors of this book will accept no responsibility, nor are they liable to any person or entity whatsoever for any injury, damage, or loss of any sort that may arise out of practicing, teaching, or disseminating of any techniques or ideas contained herein.

You assume full responsibility for the use of the information in this book and agree that the author, distributor and contributors hold no liability to you for claims, damages, costs and expenses, legal fees, or any other costs incurred due to or in any way related to your reliance on anything derived from this book or its contents.

Additionally, it is the reader's responsibility to research and comply with all local, state, and federal laws and regulations pertaining to the possession, carry, and use of self-defense weapons. This book is for educational reference information only!

Before you begin any exercise or activity, including those suggested in this book, it is important to check with your physician to see if you have any condition that might be aggravated by strenuous training. The information contained in this book is not designed to diagnose, treat, or manage any physical health conditions.

ENGAGE WITH RAGE

About This Book

Engage With Rage is designed to provide you with the knowledge, skills and attitude necessary to master clinch fighting skills and ultimately defeat your adversary in close-quarter combat.

Unlike other books on the subject, Engage With Rage is devoid of superfluous and complex maneuvers. Instead, it provides you with simple and practical tactics and techniques that can be readily applied in any high-risk self-defense situation. Keep in mind, this book addresses issues and conditions related to "real-world" self-defense scenarios. What you are about to learn is real!

Beware, some of the information and techniques contained herein are lethal and should only be used to protect yourself or a loved one from the immediate risk of unlawful criminal attack. Remember, the decision to employ physical force must always be a last resort, after all other means of avoiding violence has been thoroughly exhausted.

This book is also a skill-building workbook. So feel free to write in the margins, underline passages, and dog-ear the pages. I strongly recommend that you read this text from beginning to end, chapter by chapter. Only after you have read the entire book, should you treat it like a reference and skip around, reading those sections that interest you.

Finally, since most of the words in this text are defined within the context of the Contemporary Fighting Arts system and its related elements, I've provided a glossary of helpful terms.

Walk in peace.
Sammy Franco
ContemporaryFightingArts.com

ENGAGE WITH RAGE

INTRODUCTION
What is Contemporary Fighting Arts?

ENGAGE WITH RAGE

INTRODUCTION

Exploring Contemporary Fighting Arts

Before diving head first into this book, I'd like to first introduce you to my unique system of fighting, Contemporary Fighting Arts (CFA). I hope it will give you a greater understanding and appreciation of the material covered in this book. And for those of you who are already familiar with my CFA system, you can skip to chapter one.

Contemporary Fighting Arts® (CFA), is a state-of-the-art combat system that was introduced to the world in 1983. This sophisticated and practical system of self-defense is designed specifically to provide efficient and effective methods to avoid, defuse, confront, and neutralize both armed and unarmed assailants in a variety of deadly situations and circumstances.

Unlike karate, kung-fu, mixed martial arts and the like, CFA is the first offensive-based American martial art that is specifically designed for the violence that plagues our cruel city streets. CFA dispenses with the extraneous and the impractical and focuses on real-life street fighting.

Every technique and tactic found within the CFA system must meet three essential criteria for fighting: efficiency, effectiveness, and safety. Efficiency means that the techniques permit you to reach your combative objective quickly and economically. Effectiveness means that the elements of the system will produce the desired effect. Finally, Safety means that the combative elements provide the least amount of danger and risk for you - the fighter.

CFA is not about tournaments or senseless competition. It doesn't require you to waste time and energy practicing forms (katas) or other impractical rituals. There are no theatrical kicks or exotic techniques. Finally, CFA doesn't adhere blindly to tradition for tradition's sake. Simply put, it's a scientific yet pragmatic approach to staying alive on the streets.

CFA has been taught to people of all walks of life. Some include the U.S. Border Patrol, police officers, deputy sheriffs, security guards, military personnel, private investigators, surgeons, lawyers, college professors, airline pilots, as well as black belts, boxers, and kick boxers. CFA's broad appeal results from its ability to teach people how to really fight.

It's All In The Name

Before discussing the three components that make up Contemporary Fighting Arts, it is important to understand how CFA acquired its unique name. To begin, the first word, "Contemporary," was selected because it refers to the system's modern, up-to-date orientation. Unlike traditional martial arts, CFA is specifically designed to meet the challenges of our modern world.

The second term, "Fighting," was chosen because it accurately describes the system's combat orientation. After all, why not just call it Contemporary Martial Arts? There are two reasons for this. First, the word "martial" conjures up

INTRODUCTION

images of traditional and impractical martial art forms that are antithetical to the system. Second, why dilute a perfectly functional name when the word "fighting" defines the system so succinctly? Contemporary Fighting Arts is about teaching people how to really fight.

Let's look at the last word, "Arts." In the subjective sense, "art" refers to the combat skills that are acquired through arduous study, practice, and observation. The bottom line is that effective street fighting skills will require consistent practice and attention. Take, for example, something as seemingly basic as an elbow strike, which will actually require hundreds of hours of practice to perfect.

The pluralization of the word "Art" reflects CFA's protean instruction. The various components of CFA's training (i.e., firearms training, stick fighting, ground fighting, natural body weapon mastery, and so on) have all truly earned their status as individual art forms and, as such, require years of consistent study and practice to perfect. To acquire a greater understanding of CFA, here is an overview of the system's three vital components: the physical, the mental, and the spiritual.

The Physical Component

The physical component of CFA focuses on the physical development of a fighter, including physical fitness, weapon and technique mastery, and self-defense attributes.

Physical Fitness

If you are going to prevail in a street fight, you must be physically fit. It's that simple. In fact, you will never master the tools and skills of combat unless you're in excellent physical shape. On the average, you will have to spend more than an hour a day to achieve maximum fitness.

In CFA physical fitness comprises the following three broad

components: cardiorespiratory conditioning, muscular/skeletal conditioning, and proper body composition.

The cardiorespiratory system includes the heart, lungs, and circulatory system, which undergo tremendous stress during the course of a street fight. So you're going to have to run, jog, bike, swim, or skip rope to develop sound cardiorespiratory conditioning. Each aerobic workout should last a minimum of 30 minutes and be performed at least four times per week.

The second component of physical fitness is muscular/skeletal conditioning. In the streets, the strong survive and the rest go to the morgue. To strengthen your bones and muscles to withstand the rigors of a real fight, your program must include progressive resistance (weight training) and calisthenics. You will also need a stretching program designed to loosen up every muscle group. You can't kick, punch, ground fight, or otherwise execute the necessary body mechanics if you're "tight" or inflexible. Stretching on a regular basis will also increase the muscles' range of motion, improve circulation, reduce the possibility of injury, and relieve daily stress.

The final component of physical fitness is proper body composition: simply, the ratio of fat to lean body tissue. Your diet and training regimen will affect your level or percentage of body fat significantly. A sensible and consistent exercise program accompanied by a healthy and balanced diet will facilitate proper body composition. Do not neglect this important aspect of physical fitness.

Weapon and Technique Mastery

You won't stand a chance against a vicious assailant if you don't master the techniques of fighting. In CFA, we teach our students both armed and unarmed methods of combat. Unarmed fighting requires that you master a complete arsenal of natural body weapons and techniques. In conjunction, you must also learn the various stances, hand positioning,

INTRODUCTION

footwork, body mechanics, defensive structure, locks, chokes, and various holds. Keep in mind that something as simple as a basic punch will actually require hundreds of hours to perfect.

Range proficiency is another important aspect of weapon and technique mastery. Briefly, range proficiency is the ability to fight effectively in all three ranges of unarmed fighting. Although punching range tools are emphasized in CFA, kicking and grappling ranges cannot be neglected. Our kicking range tools consist of deceptive and powerful low-line kicks. Grappling range tools include head-butts, elbows, knees, foot stomps, biting, tearing, gouging, and crushing tactics.

Although CFA focuses on striking, we also teach our students a myriad of chokes, locks, and holds that can be used in a ground fight. While such grappling range submission techniques are not the most preferred methods of dealing with a ground fighting situation, they must be developed.

Defensive tools and skills are also taught. Our defensive structure is efficient, uncomplicated, and impenetrable. It provides the fighter maximum protection while allowing complete freedom of choice for acquiring offensive control. Our defensive structure is based on distance, parrying, blocking, evading, mobility, and stance structure. Simplicity is always the key.

Students are also instructed in specific methods of armed fighting. For example, CFA provides instruction about firearms for personal and household protection. We provide specific guidelines for handgun purchasing, operation, nomenclature, proper caliber, shooting fundamentals, cleaning, and safe storage. Our firearm program also focuses on owner responsibility and the legal ramifications regarding the use of deadly force.

CFA's weapons program also consists of natural body weapons, knives and edged weapons, single and double stick, makeshift weaponry, the side-handle baton, and oleoresin capsicum (OC) spray.

Combat Attributes

Your offensive and defensive tools are useless unless they are used strategically. For any tool or technique to be effective in a real fight, it must be accompanied by specific attributes. Attributes are qualities that enhance a particular tool, technique, or maneuver. Some examples include speed, power, timing, coordination, accuracy, non-telegraphic movement, balance, and target orientation.

CFA also has a wide variety of training drills and methodologies designed to develop and sharpen these combat attributes. For example, our students learn to ground fight while blindfolded, spar with one arm tied down, and fight while handcuffed.

Reality is the key. For example, in class students participate in full-contact drills against fully padded assailants, and real weapon disarms are rehearsed and analyzed in a variety of dangerous scenarios. Students also train with a large variety of equipment, including heavy bags, double-end bags, uppercut bags, pummel bags, focus mitts, striking shields, mirrors, rattan sticks, training bats, kicking pads, knife drones, trigger-sensitive (mock) guns, full-body armor, and numerous environmental props.

INTRODUCTION

There are more than two hundred unique training methodologies used in Contemporary Fighting Arts. Each one is scientifically designed to prepare students for the hard-core realities of real world combat. There are also three specific training methodologies used to develop and sharpen the fundamental attributes and skills of armed and unarmed fighting, including proficiency training, conditioning training, and street training.

Proficiency training can be used for both armed and unarmed skills. When conducted properly, proficiency training develops speed, power, accuracy, non-telegraphic movement, balance, and general psychomotor skill. The training objective is to sharpen one specific body weapon, maneuver, or technique at a time by executing it over and over for a prescribed number of repetitions. Each time the technique or maneuver is executed with "clean" form at various speeds. Movements are also performed with the eyes closed to develop a kinesthetic "feel" for the action. Proficiency training can be accomplished through the use of various types of equipment, including the heavy bag, double-end bag, focus mitts, training knives, real and mock pistols, striking shields, shin and knee guards, foam and plastic bats, mannequin heads, and so on.

Conditioning training develops endurance, fluidity, rhythm, distancing, timing, speed, footwork, and balance. In most cases, this type of training requires the student to deliver a variety of fighting combinations for three- or four-minute rounds separated by 30-second breaks. Like proficiency training, this type of training can also be performed at various speeds. A good workout consists of at least five rounds. Conditioning training can be performed on the bags with full-contact sparring gear, rubber training knives, focus mitts, kicking shields, and shin guards, or against imaginary assailants in shadow fighting.

Conditioning training is not necessarily limited to just three-

or four-minute rounds. For example, CFA's ground fighting training can last as long as 30 minutes. The bottom line is that it all depends on what you are training for.

Street training is the final preparation for the real thing. Since many violent altercations are explosive, lasting an average of 20 seconds, you must prepare for this possible scenario. This means delivering explosive and powerful compound attacks with vicious intent for approximately 20 seconds, resting one minute, and then repeating the process.

Street training prepares you for the stress and immediate fatigue of a real fight. It also develops speed, power, explosiveness, target selection and recognition, timing, footwork, pacing, and breath control. You should practice this methodology in different lighting, on different terrains, and in different environmental settings. You can use different types of training equipment as well. For example, you can prepare yourself for multiple assailants by having your training partners attack you with focus mitts from a variety of angles, ranges, and target postures. For 20 seconds, go after them with low-line kicks, powerful punches, and devastating strikes.

When all is said and done, the physical component creates a fighter who is physically fit and armed with an arsenal of techniques that can be deployed with destructive results.

INTRODUCTION

The Mental Component

The mental component of CFA focuses on the cerebral aspects of a fighter, developing killer instinct, strategic/tactical awareness, analysis and integration skills, philosophy, and cognitive skills.

The Killer Instinct

Deep within each of us is a cold and deadly primal power known as the "killer instinct." The killer instinct is a vicious combat mentality that surges to your consciousness and turns you into a fierce fighter who is free of fear, anger, and apprehension. If you want to survive the horrifying dynamics of real criminal violence, you must cultivate and utilize this instinctive killer mentality.

Visualization and crisis rehearsal are just two techniques used to develop, refine, and channel this extraordinary source of strength and energy so that it can be used to its full potential.

Strategic/Tactical Awareness

Strategy is the bedrock of preparedness. In CFA, there are three unique categories of strategic awareness that will diminish the likelihood of criminal victimization. They are criminal awareness, situational awareness, and self-awareness. When developed, these essential skills prepare you to assess a wide variety of threats instantaneously and accurately. Once you've made a proper threat assessment, you will be able to choose one of the following five self-defense options: comply, escape, de-escalate, assert, or fight back.

CFA also teaches students to assess a variety of other important factors, including the assailant's demeanor, intent, range, positioning and weapon capability, as well as such environmental issues as escape routes, barriers, terrain, and makeshift weaponry. In addition to assessment skills, CFA also teaches students how to enhance perception and observation skills.

Analysis and Integration Skills

The analytical process is intricately linked to understanding how to defend yourself in any threatening situation. If you want to be the best, every aspect of fighting and personal protection must be dissected. Every strategy, tactic, movement, and concept must be broken down to its atomic parts. The three planes (physical, mental, spiritual) of self-defense must be unified scientifically through arduous practice and constant exploration.

CFA's most advanced practitioners have sound insight and understanding of a wide range of sciences and disciplines. They include human anatomy, kinesiology, criminal justice, sociology, kinesics, proxemics, combat physics, emergency medicine, crisis management, histrionics, police and military science, the psychology of aggression, and the role of archetypes.

Analytical exercises are also a regular part of CFA training. For example, we conduct problem-solving sessions involving particular assailants attacking in defined environments. We move hypothetical attackers through various ranges to provide insight into tactical solutions. We scrutinize different methods of attack for their general utility in combat. We also discuss the legal ramifications of self-defense on a frequent basis.

In addition to problem-solving sessions, students are slowly exposed to concepts of integration and modification. Oral and written examinations are given to measure intellectual accomplishment. Unlike systems, CFA does not use colored belts or sashes to identify the student's level of proficiency.

Philosophy

Philosophical resolution is essential to a fighter's mental confidence and clarity. Anyone learning the art of war must find the ultimate answers to questions concerning the use of violence in defense of himself or others. To advance to the highest levels of combat awareness, you must find clear and lucid answers to such provocative questions as could you take the life of another, what are your fears, who are you, why are you interested in studying Contemporary Fighting Arts, why are you reading this book, and what is good and what is evil? If you haven't begun the quest to formulate these important questions and answers, then take a break. It's time to figure out just why you want to know the laws and rules of destruction.

Cognitive Combat Skills

Cognitive combat exercises are also important for improving one's fighting skills. CFA uses visualization and crisis rehearsal scenarios to improve general body mechanics, tools and techniques, and maneuvers, as well as tactic selection. Mental clarity, concentration, and emotional control are also developed to enhance one's ability to call upon the controlled killer instinct.

The Spiritual Component

There are many tough fighters out there. In fact, they reside in every town in every country. However, most are nothing more than vicious animals that lack self-mastery. And self-mastery is what separates the true warrior from the eternal novice.

I am not referring to religious precepts or beliefs when I speak of CFA's spiritual component. Unlike most martial arts, CFA does not merge religion into its spiritual aspect. Religion is a very personal and private matter and should never, be incorporated into any fighting system. CFA's spiritual component is not something that is taught or studied. Rather, it is that which transcends the physical and mental aspects of being and reality. There is a deeper part of each of us that is a tremendous source of truth and accomplishment.

In CFA, the spiritual component is something that is slowly and progressively acquired. During the challenging quest of combat training, one begins to tap the higher qualities of human nature. Those elements of our being that inherently enable us to know right from wrong and good from evil. As we slowly develop this aspect of our total self, we begin to strengthen qualities profoundly important to the "truth." Such qualities are essential to your growth through the mastery of inner peace, the clarity of your "vision," and your recognition of universal truths.

One of the goals of my system is to promote virtue and moral responsibility in people who have extreme capacities for physical and mental destructiveness. The spiritual component of fighting is truly the most difficult aspect of personal growth. Yet, unlike the physical component, where the practitioner's abilities will be limited to some degree by genetics and other natural factors, the spiritual component of combat offers unlimited potential for growth and development.

In the final analysis, CFA's spiritual component poses the greatest challenges for the student. It is an open-ended plane of unlimited advancement.

CHAPTER ONE
Fighting Ranges

ENGAGE WITH RAGE

FIGHTING RANGES

RANGE & DISTANCING

Before you can effectively deploy the skills and techniques found in the upcoming chapters, you must understand the concept of range or distancing. Essentially, range is the spatial relationship between you and your adversary prior to or during combat.

When assessing your opponent, you'll need to recognize the strategic implications and advantages of his range. For example, is he close enough to land a punch effectively? Or is he at a distance from which he could effectively evade your blow?

During hand-to-hand fighting, for example, there are three possible ranges from which your can launch an attack:

- *Kicking range*
- *Punching range*
- *Grappling range*

However, before discussing these fighting ranges, you must first understand the Neutral zone.

NEUTRAL ZONE

The *Neutral Zone* simply the distance at which neither you nor your assailant can strike or kick each other. The strategic implication of the neutral zone is that it creates distance between you and the assailant. This, in turn, will provide you with enhanced reaction time so that you can protect yourself adequately. Simply put, it buys you a little time.

However, don't become complacent; not all situations or environments will afford you the luxury of maintaining a neutral zone from the adversary.

From a tactical perspective, the neutral zone should be used for the following three reasons:

1. To safely assess a potential threat.
2. To de-escalate a hostile individual.
3. To assert yourself to someone from a safe distance.

KICKING RANGE

At Kicking Range, you are usually too far away to strike with your hands, so you would use your legs to strike your adversary.

In real-world combat, you should only employ low-line kicks, which are directed to targets below the assailant's waist, such as the groin, thigh, knee joint, and shinbone. Effective low-line kicks include side kicks, push kicks, hook kicks, and vertical kicks.

PUNCHING RANGE

Punching Range is the mid-range of unarmed combat. At this distance, you are close enough to strike your adversary with your hands and fists.

Punching range techniques should be quick, efficient and effective and they are the foundation of any compound attack.

FIGHTING RANGES

GRAPPLING RANGE

The third and closest range of unarmed combat is the Grappling Range, also called CQC or Close-Quarter Combat. At this distance, your assailant is too close to kick or deliver hand strikes, so you would use close-quarter strikes and techniques. For the purposes of this book, we'll be focusing exclusively on this range of combat.

Moreover, grappling range is divided into two different planes, vertical and horizontal. In the vertical plane (also know as clinch range), you can deliver impact techniques like elbow and knee strikes. In the horizontal plane of grappling range, both you and your adversary are engaged in a ground fight.

21

ENGAGE WITH RAGE

CHAPTER TWO
The Inside Position

ENGAGE WITH RAGE

UNDERSTANDING THE CLINCH

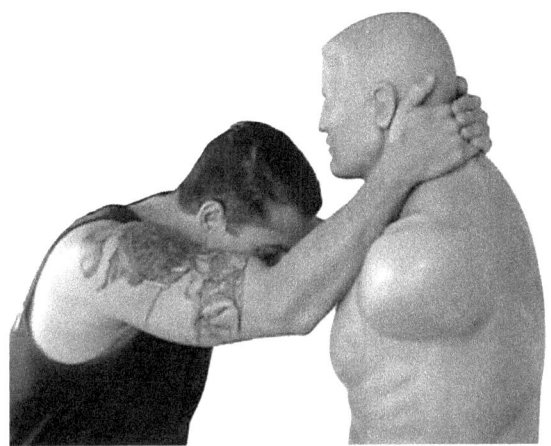

Now that you're aware of the ranges of unarmed combat, we're going to focus exclusively on grappling range and the *clinch position*.

First, *clinching* is the process of strategically locking up with your assailant while the two of you are standing up.

Second, effective clinching skills play a vital role in determining if you end up on the ground with your adversary. So if you want to avoid wrestling on the ground with your attacker (especially when fighting multiple attackers) then you must know how to fight in the clinch and ultimately control it.

Remember, the clinch is the last range of combat before the two of you go to the ground. So if you don't use this golden opportunity to neutralize your adversary, you can bet that the both of you are going to end up on the ground. And the ground is one of the worst places to be when engaged in a real-world self-defense situation. I've discussed these ground fighting vulnerabilities ad nauseam in many of my other books.

Interestingly enough, most violent confrontations invariably end up with the two combatants locked up in some sort of temporary clinch. Very seldom is it the result of strategic planning, more often it's the physical residual of two forces fueled by adrenaline and rage who collide into one another. Whatever its cause, the clinch is a very real element of street combat that must be mastered if you are to survive.

Did you know that many (pre-contact stage) street altercations begin at grappling or clinching range? The irony is that most people don't have a clue what to do at this distance of engagement. In this photo, the aggressor (left) encroaches upon the defender (right).

THE BIG ADVANTAGE OF CLINCHING

The biggest advantage to mastering clinch fighting is that most people don't know how to fight in this range. The average person on the street might know how to throw a punch or two, but they become lost when forced to fight at close-quarters. I know this from firsthand experience, when I've forced my adversary into a clinch position. They immediately become panic stricken. It's human nature to fear the unknown.

Ironically, even in combat sports like boxing, when two boxers are locked up in a clinch, they're immediately separated by the referee. Clinch fighting is taboo.

THE INSIDE POSITION

DEFENSIVE CLINCHING

While this book is primarily devoted to offensive clinching, I should mention that clinching can be used for defensive purposes. For example, clinching can be employed immediately after you have performed a specific defensive technique such as a block, parry, stiff-arm jam, webbing technique, etc. With defensively clinching, you negate the opponent's ability to maintain his offensive flow. The objective is to bypass his assault and re-establish offensive control.

For instance, imagine your adversary attacks you with an upper body tackle. To thwart his assault, you can immediately negate his attempted takedown with a stiff-arm jam and move into a clinch position to stabilize your balance and establish a dominant inside position. Once in the clinch position, you counter the adversary with a series of head butts, knee strikes and elbows until he is sufficiently neutralized.

The following sequence of photos demonstrate defensive clinching in action.

Step 1: In this photo, the man (left) attempts a body tackle.

Step 2: The practitioner (right) immediately lowers his height to match the opponent's level of entry, and negates the forward momentum with a stiff-arm jam to the upper chest region.

Step 3: Once the stiff-arm jam negates the opponent's momentum, the defender (right) rushes in and engages the defensive clinch position.

THE INSIDE POSITION

Step 4: The defender switches to offense, and immediately counters with a head butt strike to the assailant's nose.

Pictured below, another example of defensive clinching. Here, the defender (left) blocks a haymaker punch, immediately engages the clinch, and counters with a knee strike to the groin.

a

b

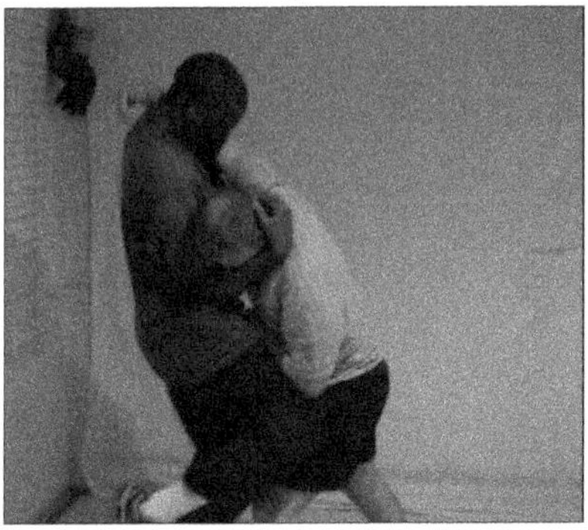

c

d

HOW TO CLINCH

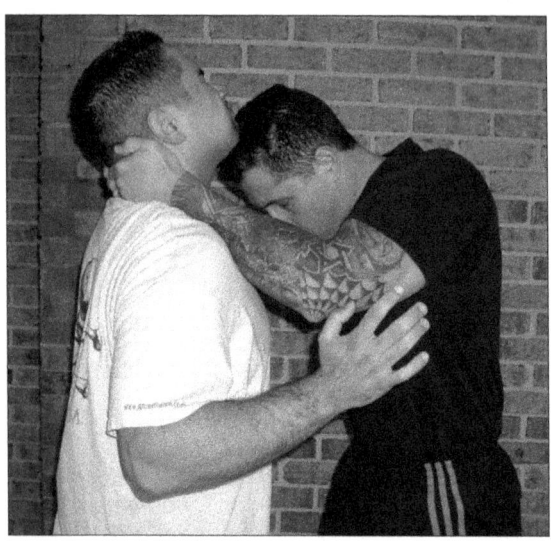

A strong well-balanced stance is one of the most overlooked elements of proper clinching skills. The sad fact is many fighters place too little emphasis on their stance when they lock up with their opponents. Keep in mind, if your stance is flawed, your balance will be lost, and your clinch will most likely fall apart during the fight.

HOW TO STAND WHEN CLINCHING

To assume the proper stance when clinching with your adversary, blade your feet and body at approximately 45-degrees from the opponent. This moves your body targets back and away from direct strikes, but still leaves you strategically positioned to attack.

Next, place your feet approximately shoulder-width apart with both knees bent and flexible. Your body weight must be equally distributed over both feet. Let your bodyweight sink into the ground.

Place both of your hands on the back of the opponent's

neck, clamp down hard and be certain that your hands overlap each other. Finally, keep your chin slightly angled down. Remember to always be cognizant of your weight distribution when clinching, if you lose your balance, you're screwed.

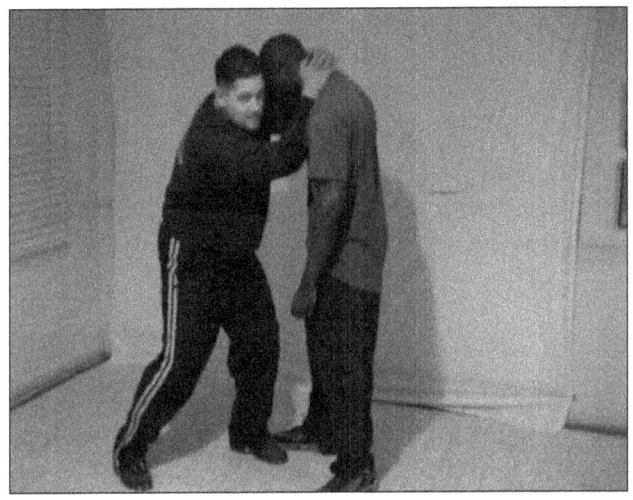

A solid stance is a vital component of effective clinching.

THE NECK CLAMP

Once you establish the clinch position, it's equally important to maintain it. The most important aspect of controlling the clinch is to employ the proper hand gripping technique. This type of neck hold is essential. If you can effectively control the opponent's head in the clinch, you will ultimately control his body.

While mixed martial art styles teach a wide variety of clinch positions, in my Contemporary Fighting Arts (CFA) system, there's only one way that really matters in an emergency self-defense situation. I refer to it as the "neck clamp".

To assume the neck clamp, start by placing both of your hands on the back of the opponent's neck, clamp down hard and be certain that your hands overlap each other. Remember to tuck your elbows in to protect against body shots.

ENGAGE WITH RAGE

Once your hands secure the opponent's neck, pull down forcefully. Don't just pull with your arms; remember to use your entire body to control him. Keep everything tight!

Also, make certain that both of your forearms run over his collarbone. This will significantly enhance your leverage.

Avoid becoming too tense when clinching with your adversary. You need to be able to feel his weight, balance and energy shift during the fight. It's also important not to interlace your fingers when grasping the back of the opponent's neck. Also remember that the inside position is particularly effective against taller opponents.

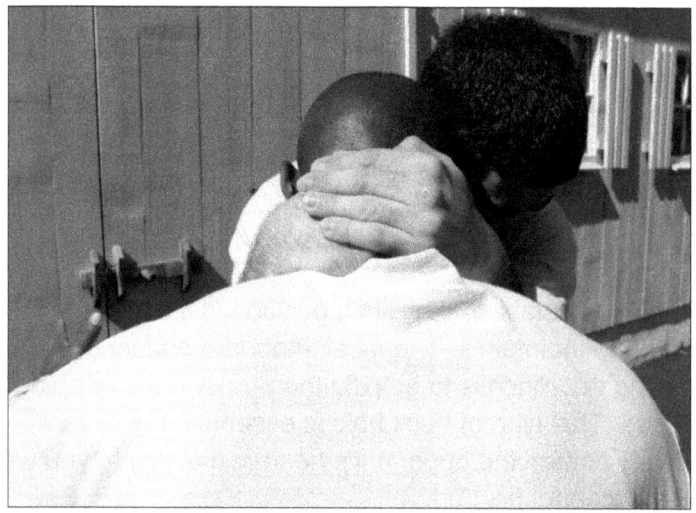

Pictured here, the proper way to control the adversary in the clinch. Remember, place both of your hands on the back of the opponent's neck, clamp down hard and be certain that your hands overlap each other.

THE INSIDE POSITION

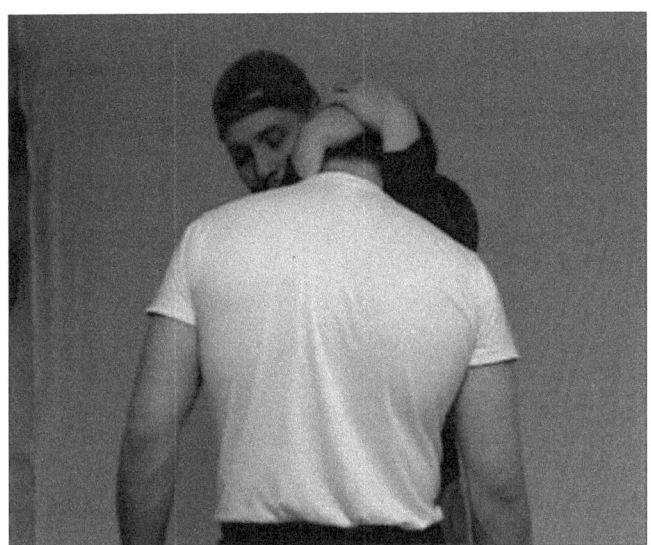

Avoid grasping the top of the opponent's head, as it provide poor control of the opponent. Always control his neck.

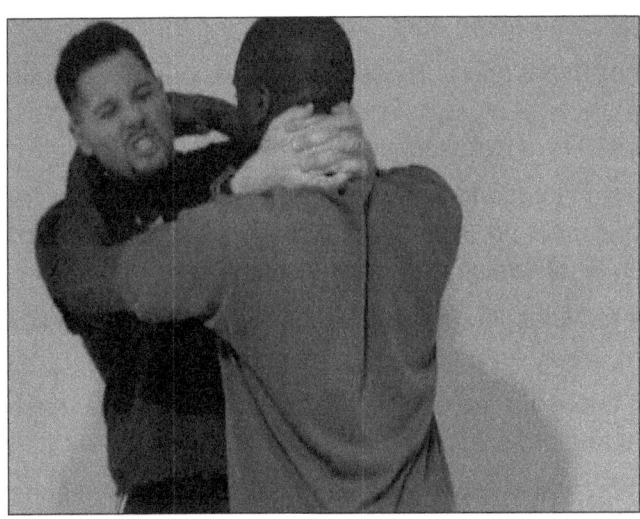

When grasping the opponent's neck, never interlace your fingers. First, it lock up you fingers. Second, the opponent can bend his head back and pinch your fingers together. Ouch!

THE INSIDE POSITION

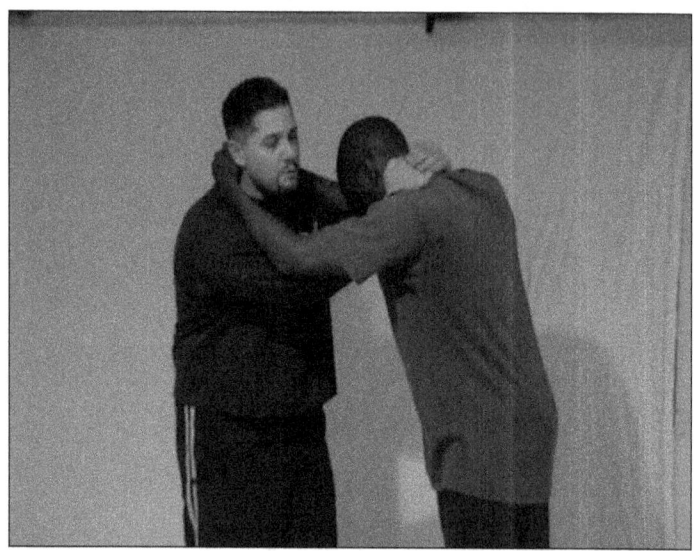

Once you've mastered both the proper stance and neck clamp technique, it's time to learn about the *inside position*. This is particularly important when both you and your adversary are locked up in a clinch during the fight.

For all intent and purposes, the *inside position* simply means that both of your hands are inside of your opponent's arms when he's clinched with you.

The advantage to acquiring and maintaining the inside position cannot be overstated. Here are just a few reasons why you want this strategic arm positioning:

1. It provides the greatest amount of leverage and control over the adversary.

2. It opens up the opponent's centerline, thereby exposing vital anatomical targets.

3. It facilitates rapid deployment of striking techniques from the clinch position.

4. If necessary, it permits you to quickly trap the assailant's limbs.

THE INSIDE POSITION

Pictured here, Franco demonstrates the tremendous amount of leverage and control you have over the adversary when utilizing the inside clinch position.

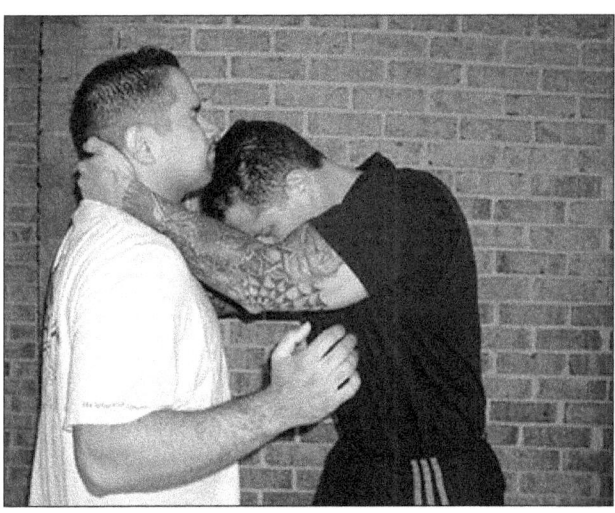

The inside position provides quick deployment of striking techniques from the clinch. Here, Franco delivers a face-shattering head but strike.

CLINCH SWIMMING DRILL

The swimming drill is a great exercise for helping you and your partner become acquainted with the clinch as well the proper technique for acquiring the inside position.

Step 1: Face your training partner at the grappling range with both of your bodies angled slightly. Stretch you arms forward and place both of your hands on your partner's neck. Have your partner place his arms on the inside of your arms with his hands clasped around your neck (the "inside position").

Step 2: Take your left hand off your partner's neck, bring it under and inside his outstretched arm and clasp the back of his neck.

THE INSIDE POSITION

Step 3: Next, do the same with your right arm. You will now have the inside position and your partner has the outside position.

Now, it's your training partner's turn to acquire the inside position. Have him follow the same steps that you just performed. Remember to move one arm at a time and use your legs and body to force your training partner backwards as you snake your arms into the inside position.

This is a fluid drill, so pay close attention to your form and remain balanced at all times. Once you and your partner get the hang of this swimming motion, you can incorporate various close quarter strikes (i.e., knee strikes, vertical elbows, head butts, etc).

ENGAGE WITH RAGE

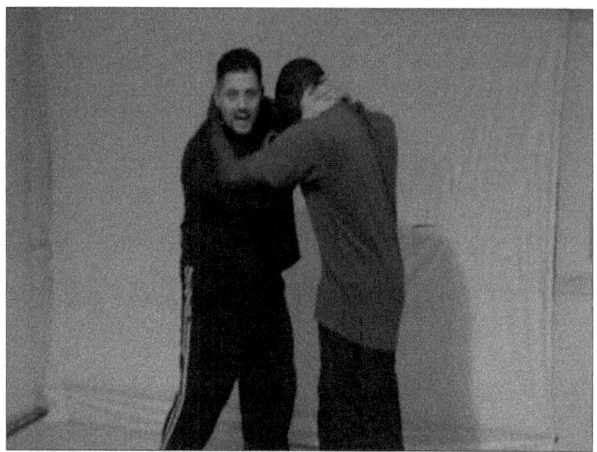

Here, Franco demonstrates the inside position.

SOLO SWIMMING DRILL

Practicing the swimming drill with a partner is ideal. However, not everyone has the luxury of a training partner. Fortunately, you can practice the swimming drill with the body opponent bag.

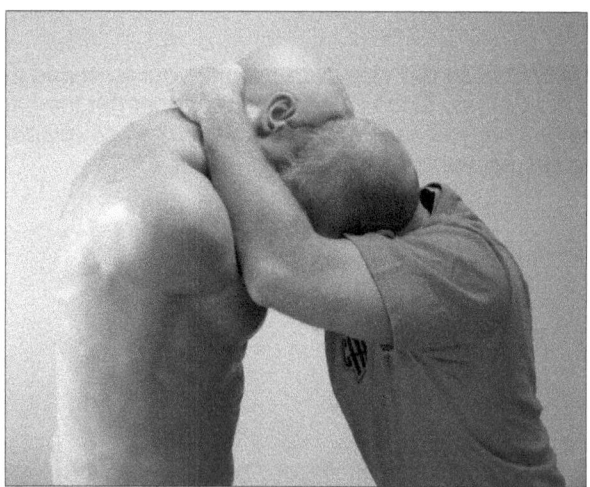

If you don't have a training partner, the Body Opponent Bag is a great tool for working on your clinching techniques. The next page demonstrates how to swim with the body opponent bag.

ANCHORING THE AGGRESSOR

From left to right, a basic solo swimming sequence.

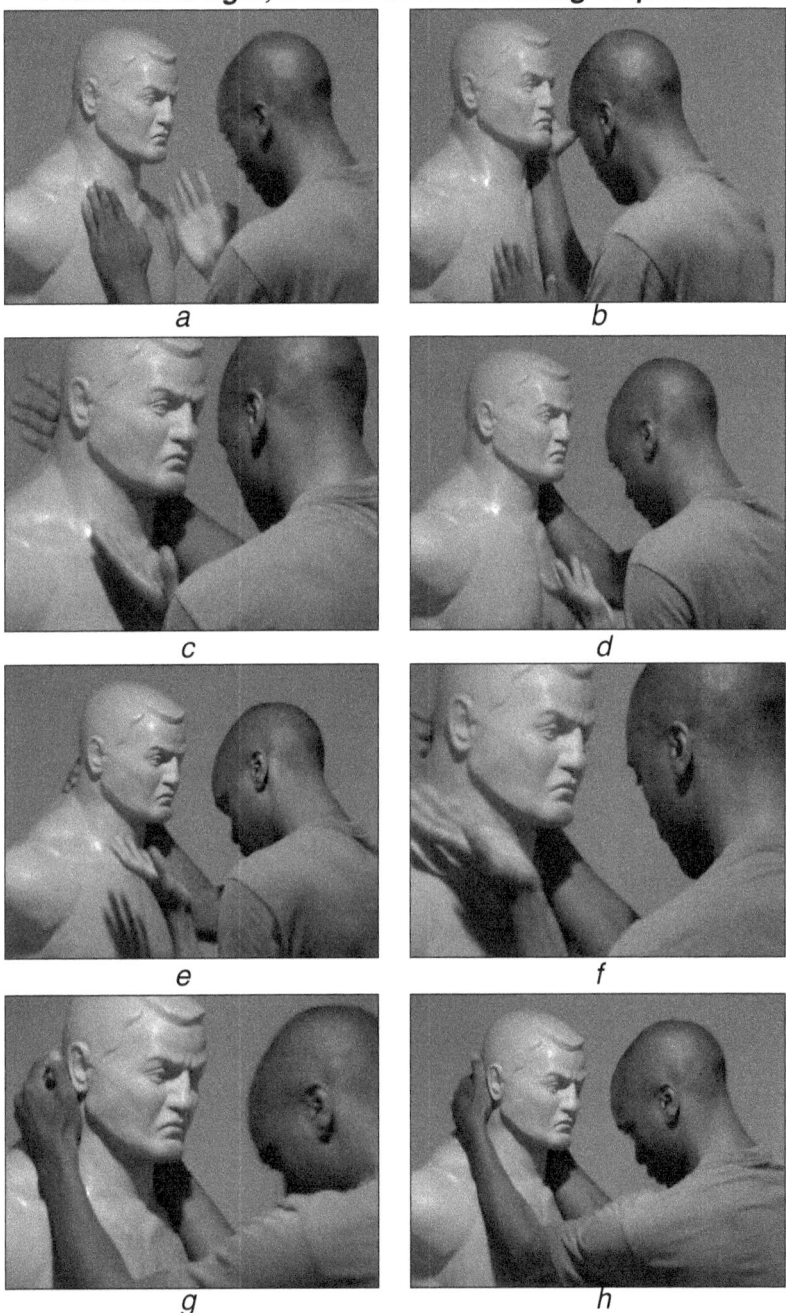

HALF-CLINCH POSITION

While there are many different types of clinch positions, the two hand inside position is the best for practical self-defense and it's what we're going to focus on exclusively in this book.

However, it's worth giving a brief mention to the half-clinch position. Essentially, the half-clinch position is a transitory clinch hold, where only one of your arms has acquired the inside position. While not an ideal position for effective clinch fighting, there are some techniques that can be applied from here.

What follows on the next page is just one example...

ANCHORING THE AGGRESSOR

Biceps Choke from Half-Clinch Position

Start from the half-clinch position.

Next, slap the opponent's right arm upwards.

Simultaneously drop your head under the opponent's arm.

Shoot your right arm past the opponent's neck.

Feed your right hand into the crook of your left arm. Bring your left hand back to your ear.

Complete the biceps choke by scissoring both of your arms together.

HUBOD FLOW DRILL

You can improve your clinch fighting skills by adding flow drills to your training. Flow drills are excellent for developing timing, speed and proper hand placement. Here are a few exercises to get you started.

Step: 1: The two men begin the hubod drill with the man on the left initiating a tight overhead strike. The man on the right blocks the hit.

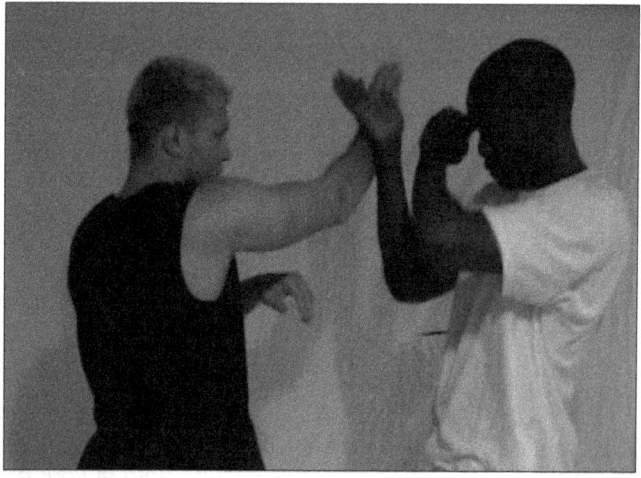

Step 2: After blocking the strike, the man (right) uses his right arm to redirect his partner's striking arm.

ANCHORING THE AGGRESSOR

Step 3: As the man on the right redirects his partner's arm, he slaps it downward with his left hand.

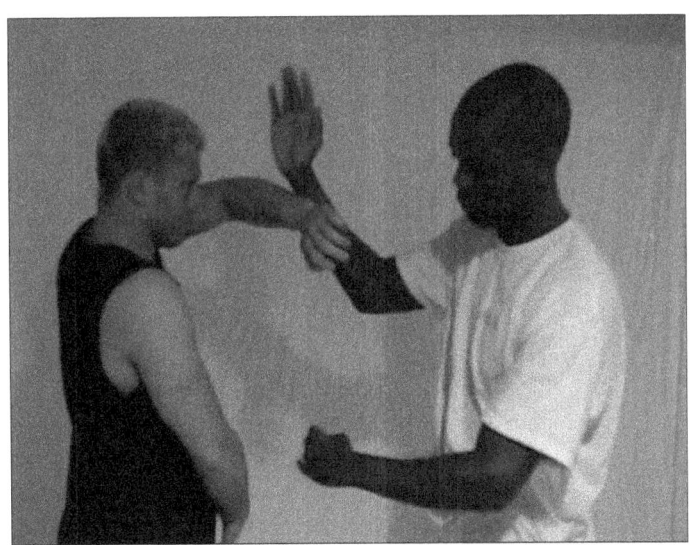

Step 4: Next, the man on the right attacks his partner with a tight overhead strike.

ENGAGE WITH RAGE

Step 5: The man on the left blocks his partner's strike and redirects it with his right arm.

Step 6: As he redirects his partner's arm, he slaps it downward with his left hand.

ANCHORING THE AGGRESSOR

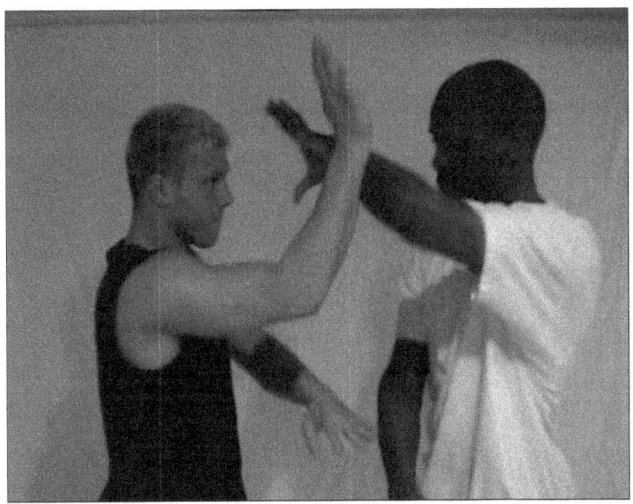

Step 7: The cycle is complete and the man on the left begins again with a tight overhead strike. The drill continues back and forth.

ENGAGING THE CLINCH FLOW DRILL

Next, we're going to integrate the clinch position within the hubod drill. This action is done arbitrarily between the training partners. Remember, keep the drill alive and fluid.

Step: 1: The two men begin the drill with the man on the left initiating a tight overhead strike. The man on the right blocks it.

ENGAGE WITH RAGE

Step 2: After blocking the hit, the man on the right uses his right arm to redirect his partner's striking arm.

Step 3: As the man on the right redirects his partners arm and slaps it downward with his left hand.

ANCHORING THE AGGRESSOR

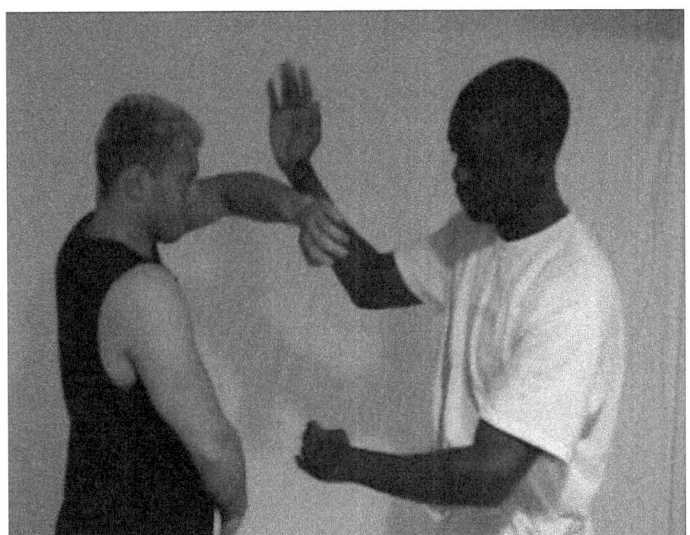

Step 4: Next, the man on the right strikes his partner with a tight overhead strike.

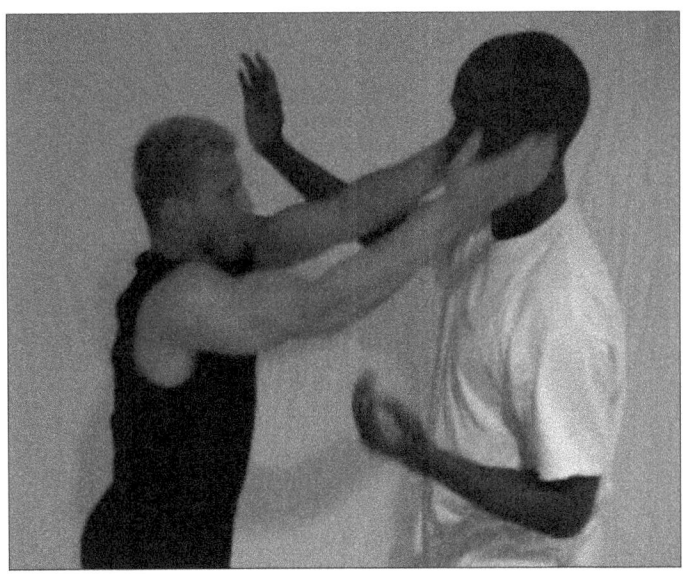

Step 5: The man on the left blocks the strike and launches himself into the clinch position.

ENGAGE WITH RAGE

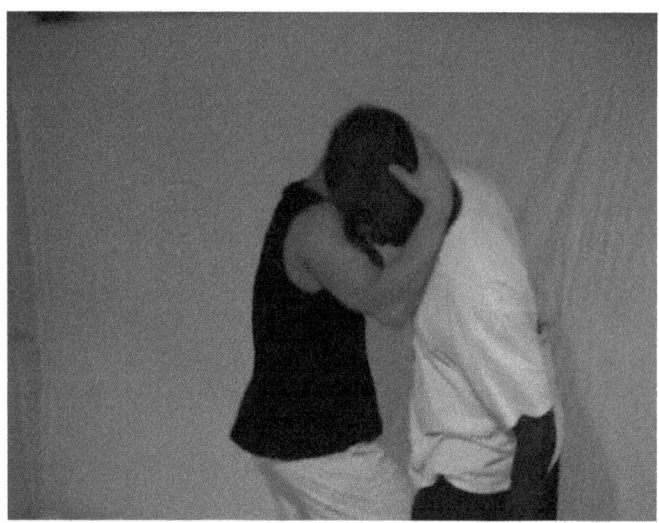

Step 6: He locks up in the clinch position.

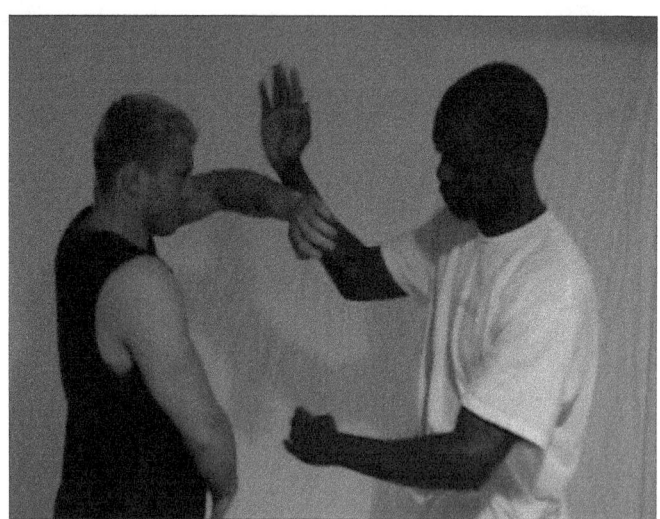

Step 7: The drill continues. The man on the right attacks his partner with a tight overhead strike.

ANCHORING THE AGGRESSOR

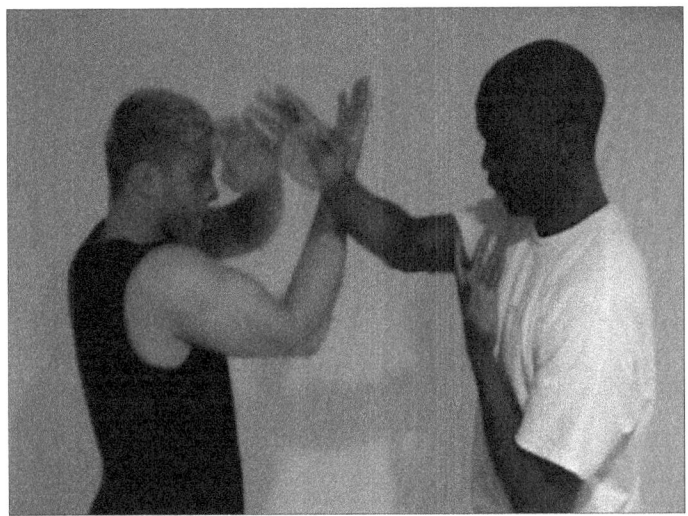

Step 8: The man on the left blocks his partner's strike and redirects it with his right arm.

Step 9: As he redirects his partner's arm, he slaps it downward with his left hand.

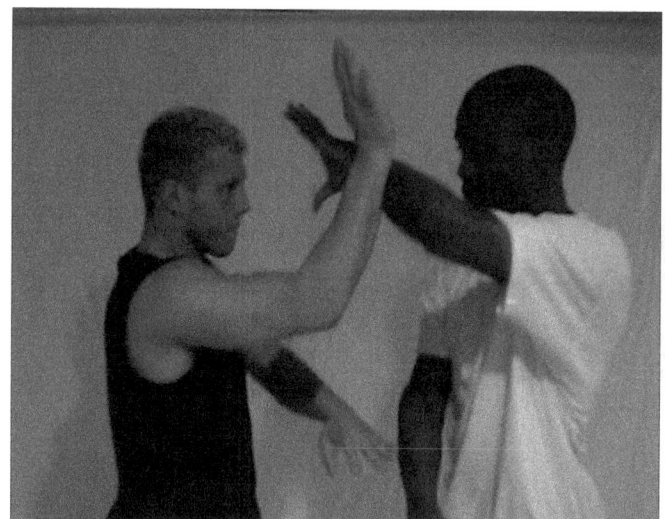

Step 10: The man on the left attacks with a tight overhead strike, the man on the right blocks the strike, and...

Step 11: Launches himself into the clinch position.

ANCHORING THE AGGRESSOR

Step 12: He follows up with a simulated head butt strike.

ENGAGE WITH RAGE

CHAPTER THREE
Anchoring the Aggressor

ENGAGE WITH RAGE

ANCHORING THE AGGRESSOR

WHAT IS ANCHORING?

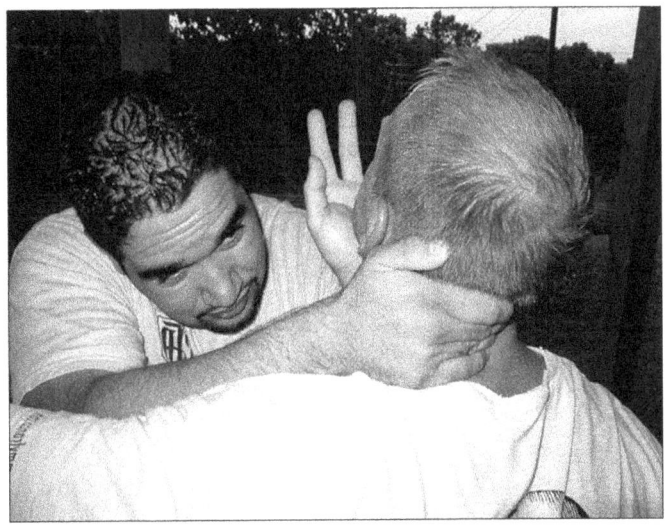

In order to successfully deploy the bulk of your clinch fighting techniques, you're going to have to let go of one hand from the neck clamp. This is when *Anchoring* comes into play.

In my original book, *The Widow Maker Program: Extreme Self-Defense for Deadly Force Situations*, I discussed the critical importance of anchoring the opponent during the *razing* method of attack. This tactic is vital and certainly worth reviewing for the purposes of this book.

Essentially, anchoring means controlling and preventing the adversary from disengaging the range of engagement when you're attacking. Remember, in order for your close-quarter offensive techniques to work effectively, you must maintain close-quarter combat range and <u>keep the pressure on the adversary</u>.

There are two variations of anchoring that you'll need to be familiar with: offense and defense. Let's look at each one.

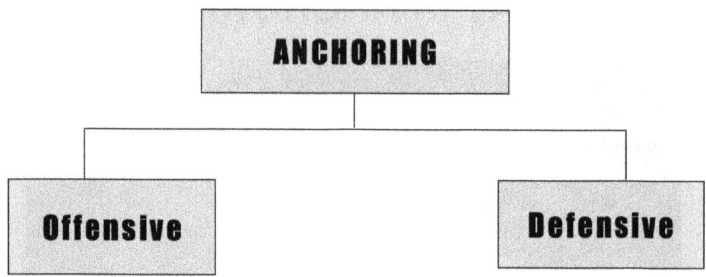

The two variations of anchoring: offensive and defensive.

OFFENSIVE ANCHORING

Offenses anchoring is pretty much self explanatory, requiring you to grab hold of your opponent's neck with one hand while performing the various close-quarter offensive technique with your other free hand.

Offensive anchoring is critical for the following five reasons:

1. It maintains the clinch range for effective and continuous offensive assault.

2. It prevents the opponent from disengaging close-quarter combat range.

3. It stabilizes the assailant's head allowing maximum pressure against all facial targets.

4. It provides a tactile reference point, in case your vision is somehow impaired during the course of the fight.

5. It transmits an alpha or predator body language to the enemy.

ANCHORING THE AGGRESSOR

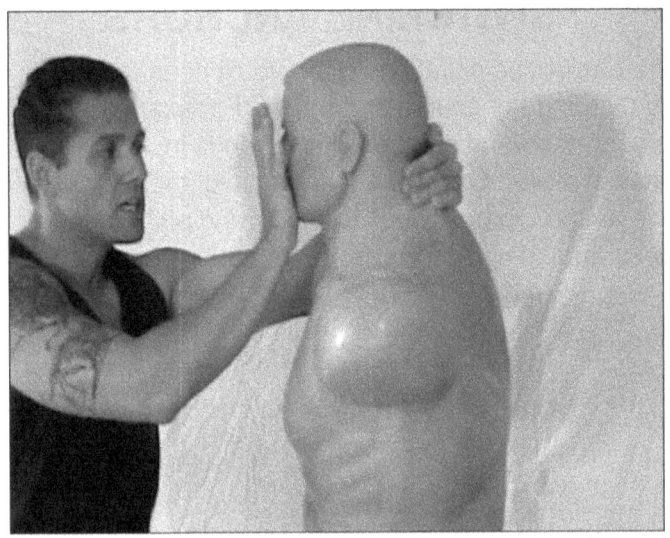

Offensive anchoring requires you to release one of your hands from the two-handed clinch position. To avoid injuring your thumb when anchoring your opponent, always keep your thumb securely tucked down against his neck.

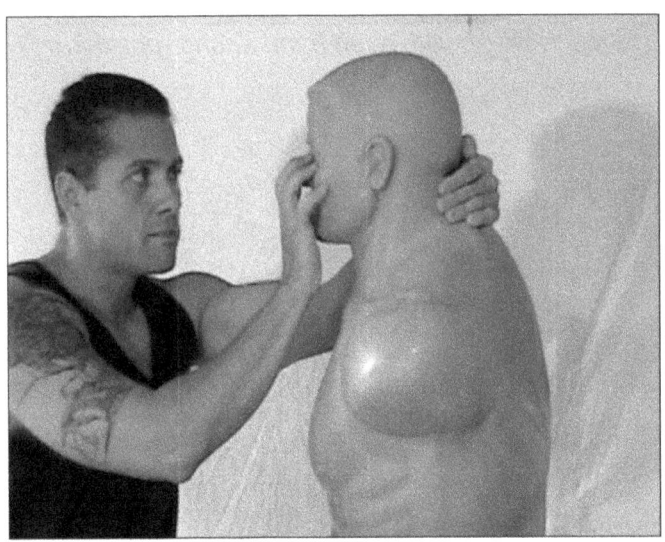

Once your anchor is secure, you can begin attacking with your free hand.

SWITCHING ANCHORS

There might be situations when you'll need to switch anchors during the course of the fight. For example, you might injure your hand and need to switch hands in order to maintain the offensive flow. Or, your adversary might force you to change anchoring positions. The following photo sequence demonstrate the correct way to switch neck anchors.

Step 1: Begin with a left hand anchor position.

Step 2: Remove your left anchor and simultaneously attack the opponent with both of your hands.

ANCHORING THE AGGRESSOR

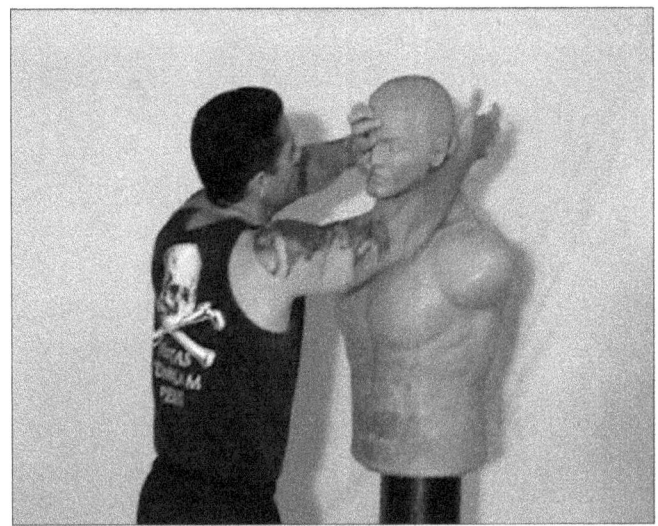

Step 3: While maintaining offensive pressure, move your right hand behind the opponent's neck.

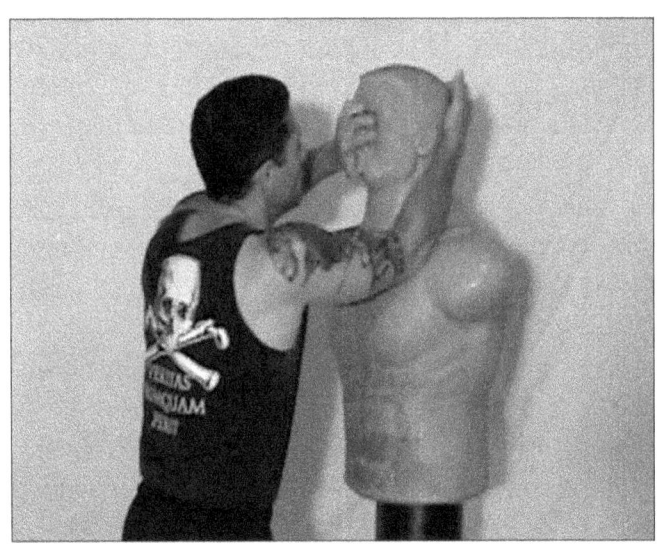

Step 4: Firmly secure the opponent's neck while continuing to assault him with your left hand.

DEFENSIVE ANCHORING

Next, is *defensive anchoring*, which is used when your offensive flow is broken and the opponent retaliates with a barrage of strikes to your head.

Defensive anchoring requires you to grab hold of the opponent's neck with both of your hands (neck clamp) while dropping your head between both of your biceps. Defensive anchoring is a temporary protective posture that hides your head and nullifies the opponent's strikes.

Best of all, it still enables you to control the opponent and prevent him from disengaging the range of engagement. The objective is to protect your head from the attack until you can regain control of the opponent's arms.

If you're concerned about receiving debilitating blows to your stomach, not to worry. The downward force of the neck clamp significantly negates the opponent's punching leverage. Nevertheless, if you're still concerned, try tensing your abdominal muscles and expelling air from your lungs if punches make contact. You can also add abdominal conditioning exercises and impact training to strengthen your lower body to withstand body blows.

ANCHORING THE AGGRESSOR

Franco demonstrates the proper hand positioning (neck clamp) required for defensive anchoring.

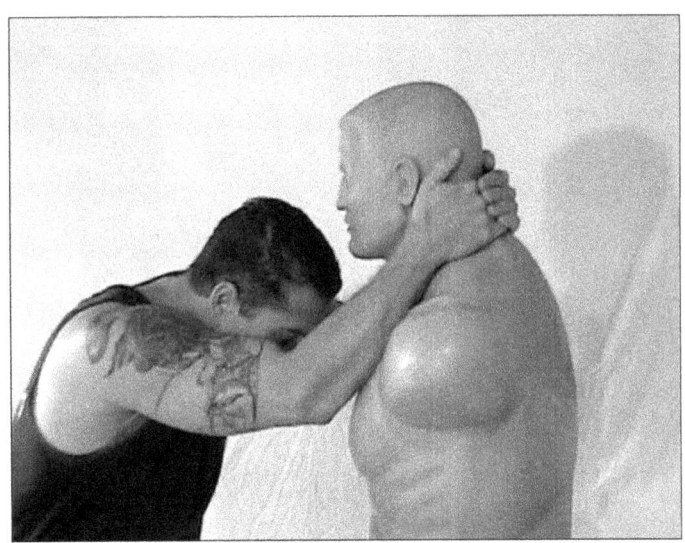

Notice how he drops his head down between his biceps to avoid and deflect possible blows.

ENGAGE WITH RAGE

In the following photo sequence, notice how the attacker's blows (right) are nullified when the defender tucks his head down and anchors the opponent's neck.

a

b

ANCHORING THE AGGRESSOR

TWO ANCHOR POINTS

The ideal anchoring point is the opponent's neck because it provides the greatest amount of stability and control. However, under some circumstances, you can also anchor the opponent's upper arm.

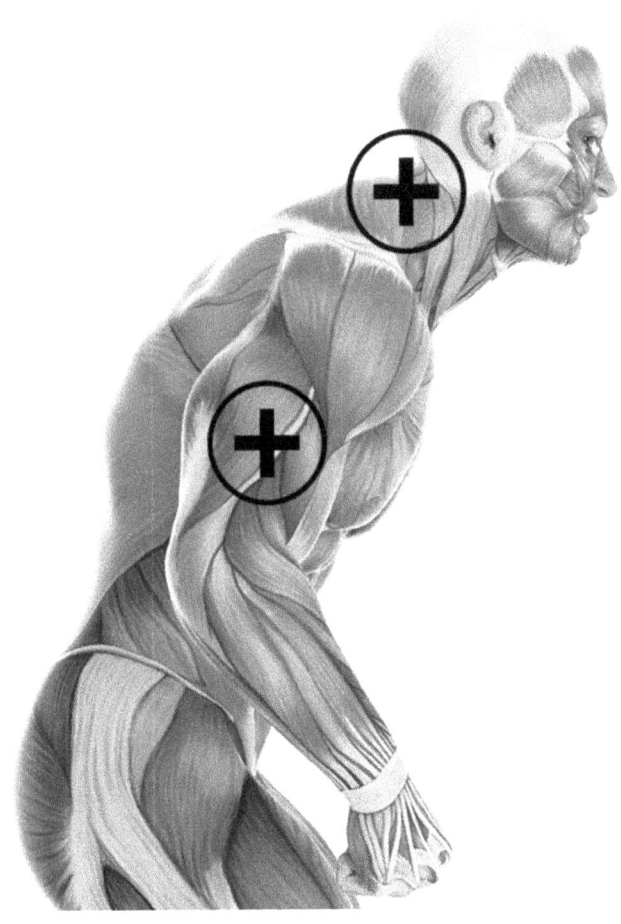

ANCHORING THE UPPER ARM

Anchoring the opponent's upper arm is a tactic used to transition from a defensive anchor back to offense. To accomplish this, release one of your hands from the defensive anchor position, intercept the opponent's swinging upper arm, and trap it. Once you've anchored his arm, you'll have the freedom to counterattack. Take a look at the following arm anchoring demonstration.

Here, the defender (left) maintains a defensive anchor.

The opponent (right) continues to swing wildly.

ANCHORING THE AGGRESSOR

The defender is safe and sound as his opponent continues his feckless assault.

At the proper moment, the defender wraps his left arm (windmill motion) around his opponent's right arm.

ENGAGE WITH RAGE

Once the defender traps his opponent's upper right arm, he uses it as an anchor point, and begins his counterattack with his right hand.

He continues his counterattack until his adversary is neutralized.

CHAPTER FOUR
Target Areas & Techniques

ENGAGE WITH RAGE

TARGETS INSIDE THE CLINCH

In order to dominate the adversary from the clinch, we must first discuss specific targets that will be available to you from this strategic position.

As discussed in many of my previous books, the assailant's anatomical targets are located in one of three possible *target zones*.

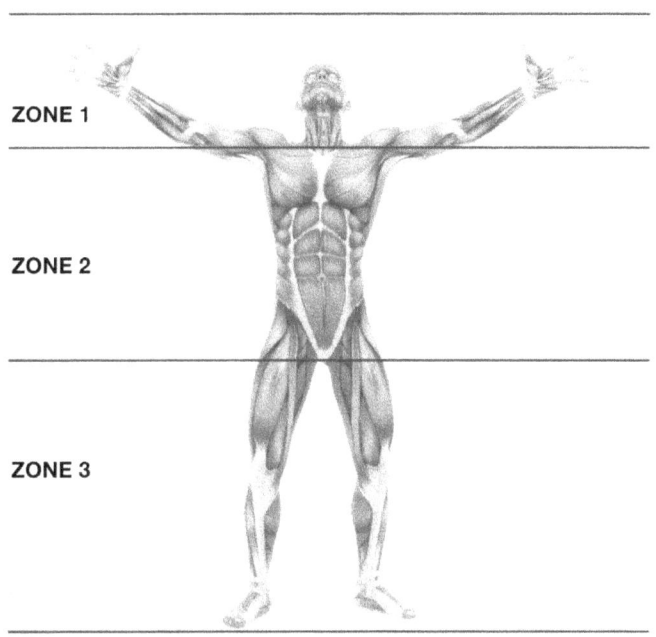

Zone 1: (head region) consists of targets related to the assailant's senses, including the eyes, temples, nose, chin, and back of neck.

Zone 2: (neck, torso, groin) consists of targets related to the assailant's breathing, including the throat, solar plexus, ribs, and groin.

Zone 3: (legs and feet) consists of anatomical targets related to the assailant's mobility, including the thighs, knees, shins, insteps, and toes.

For clinch combat, <u>there's going be a limited amount of targets at your disposal</u>. Eight of them, to be exact. Let's take a good look at these targets and the medical implications associated with each of them.

EYES

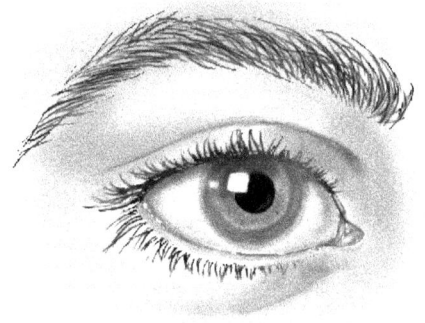

Eyes sit in the orbital of the skull. They're ideal targets for clinch fighting because they are one of the most important organs for your assailant to effectively fight. Not to mention that the eyes are extremely sensitive and difficult to protect. Also striking them requires minimal force.

The eyes can be poked, scratched, and gouged from a variety of angles and vantages. Depending on the force of your strike, it can cause numerous injuries, including watering of the eyes, hemorrhaging, blurred vision, temporary or permanent blindness, severe pain, rupture, shock, and even unconsciousness

TARGET AREAS & TECHNIQUES

EARS

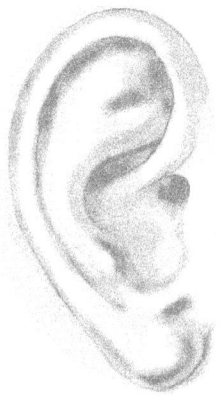

Like the eyes, the ears are extremely sensitive to attack from the clinch position. The opponent's ears can be punched, popped and torn. When struck with a moderate amount of force, the tympanic membrane (eardrum) will easily rupture.

Striking the ear can also result in percussive shock, extreme pain, unconsciousness, partial or complete loss of hearing, bleeding, disorientation, and loss of balance.

You can use the following body weapons to attack the ears: cupped palm strike, elbow strikes, and fingers.

TEMPLE

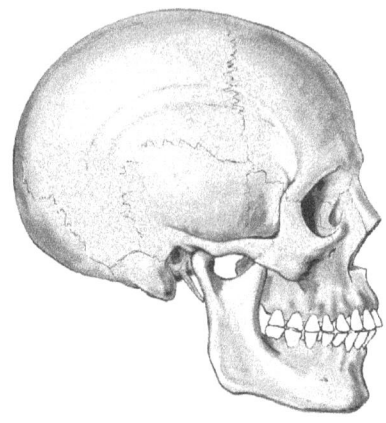

The temple or sphenoid bone is a thin, weak bone located on both sides of the skull approximately one inch from the assailant's eye. Because of its inherently weak structure and close proximity to the brain, a very powerful strike to this anatomical target can be deadly.

Other possible injuries include unconsciousness, hemorrhage, concussion, shock, and coma. You can use your elbows and forehead to strike the assailant's temple from the clinch position.

TARGET AREAS & TECHNIQUES

NOSE

The nose is made up of a thin bone, cartilage, numerous blood vessels, and many nerves. It is a particularly good impact target because it stands out from the assailant's face and can be struck from three different directions (up, straight, down).

A moderate blow can cause stunning pain, eye watering, temporary blindness, and hemorrhaging. A powerful strike can result in shock and unconsciousness.

Palm jolts, hammer fists, and elbow strikes can be delivered effectively to the assailant's nose from the clinch position.

CHIN

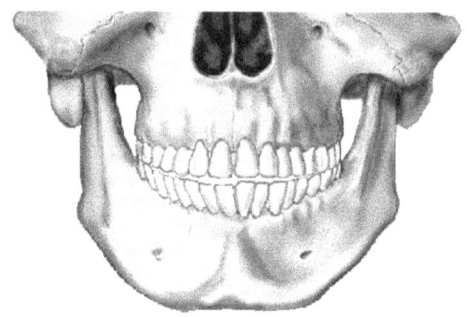

The chin is a great target for clinch fighting. When the chin is struck at a forty-five degree angle, shock waves are transmitted to the cerebellum and cerebral hemispheres of the brain, resulting in paralysis and immediate unconsciousness. Depending on the force of your blow, other possible injuries include broken jaw, concussion, and whiplash to the assailant's neck.

Some of the best body weapons to strike the chin are: elbow strikes, palm jolts, and head butts.

BACK OF NECK

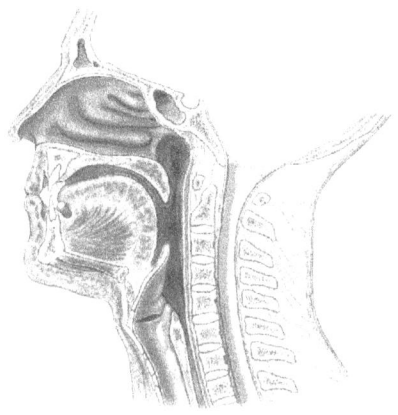

The back of the assailant's neck consists of the first seven vertebrae (also called the cervical vertebrae) of the spinal column. They function as a circuit board for nerve impulses from the brain to the body. The back of the neck is a lethal target because the vertebrae are poorly protected.

A very powerful strike to the back of the assailant's neck can cause shock, unconsciousness, a broken neck, complete paralysis, coma, and death. The best body weapons to attack the cervical vertebra are hammer fists, elbow strikes, and neck cranks.

THROAT

In a do-or-die self-defense situation, attacking your assailant's throat can save your life. The throat is considered a lethal target because a thin layer of skin only protects it. This region consists of the thyroid, hyaline, and crocoid cartilage, trachea, and larynx. The trachea, or windpipe, is a cartilaginous cylindrical tube that measures 4 ½ inches in length and approximately one inch in diameter.

A direct and powerful strike to this target may result in unconsciousness, blood drowning, massive hemorrhaging, air starvation, and death. If the thyroid cartilage is crushed, hemorrhaging will occur, the windpipe will quickly swell shut, and the assailant will die of suffocation.

TARGET AREAS & TECHNIQUES

THIGHS

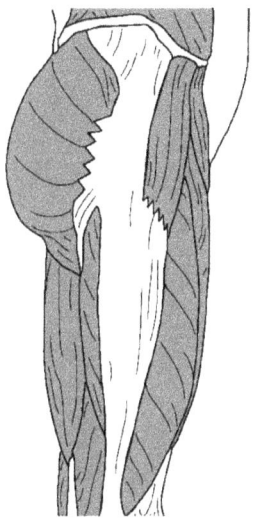

Don't overlook the thighs as an impact target. In fact, because the thighs are a large and difficult to protect, they make excellent striking targets from the clinch position.

While you can attack the thighs at a variety of different angles, the ideal location is the assailant's common peroneal nerve located on the side of the thigh, approximately four inches above the knee. Striking this area can result in extreme pain and immediate immobility of the afflicted leg. An extremely hard strike to the thigh may result in a fracture of the femur, internal bleeding, severe pain, intense cramping, and long-term immobility.

CLINCH TECHNIQUES

Now that you're aware of anchoring and the various clinch targets, it's time to teach you the specific offensive techniques that can be applied in this range. They include:

1. Head butt
2. Raking
3. Gouging
4. Biting
5. Palm jolt
6. Hammer fist
7. Elbow strike
8. Shaving forearm
9. Bicep pop
10. Knee strike
11. Neck crank
12. Finishing choke

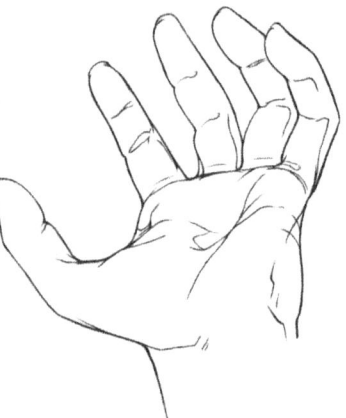

HEAD BUTT

TARGET AREAS & TECHNIQUES

There's a very good reason the head butt is illegal in sport combat competitions... it's a brutal strike that can cause a massive amount of damage!

The Head Butt is also the number one striking technique inside the clinch, because it doesn't require you to relinquish control of the assailant's neck when delivering the blow.

While the head butt can be delivered in four different directions (forward, backward, right side, and left side), you'll want to focus on forward striking when clinch fighting.

Accuracy is critical. When delivering a forward head butt, make certain to strike with the top portion of your head (frontal bone) against the opponent's facial targets, such as the nose, temple, chin, upper middle mandibular joint, and orbital bones.

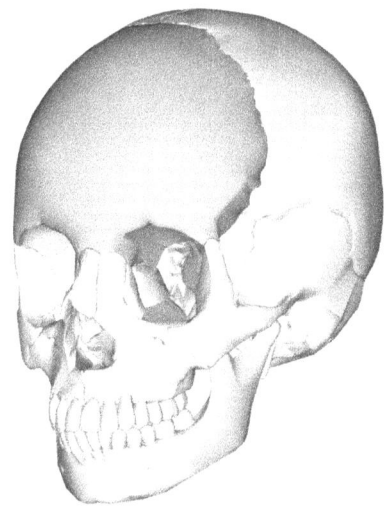

Pictured here, the frontal bone, which is the strongest part of the human skull. Notice the large surface area that can be used for striking weaker facial targets.

Essentially, there are two types of head butts that can be delivered in a forward direction, and they will largely depend on the height of the adversary. Keep in mind, the *neck clamp* technique (discussed in the previous chapter), will often afford you the leverage to adjust the height of the opponent's facial targets. The two types of forward head butt strikes include:

Clipping - This type of head butt is delivered in a downward whipping motion, and it's primarily used against adversaries who are the same hight or shorter.

Ramming - This head butt is delivered in an upward ramming motion against opponent's who are taller than you.

Pictured here, the clipping head butt, targeting for the nose.

The ramming head butt, targeting the chin.

TARGET AREAS & TECHNIQUES

HEAD BUTT DRILL

In this training exercise, we're going to integrate the head butt with the swimming drill that was discussed in chapter two.

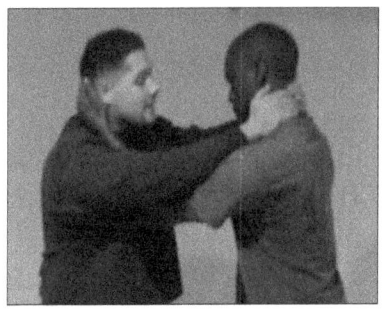

1. Franco starts the drill from the outside position.

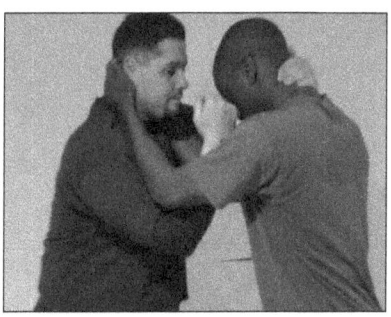

2. First, he inserts his right arm inside the opponent's arm.

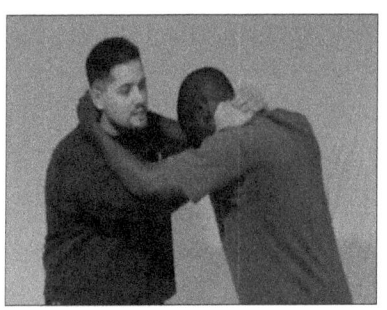

3. Next, he moves his left arm inside his opponent's arm.

4. From the inside position, he simulates a head butt strike.

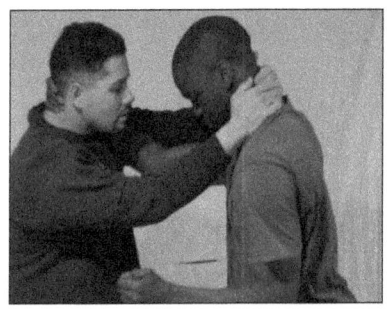

5. Franco's partner begins the swimming drill.

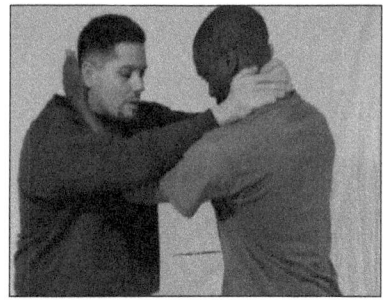

6. He swims his left arm inside Franco's arm.

ENGAGE WITH RAGE

7. Next, he swims his right arm inside Franco's arm.

8. From the inside position, he simulates a head butt strike.

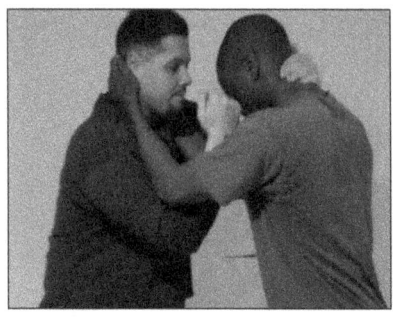

9. Franco swims his right arm inside the opponent's arm.

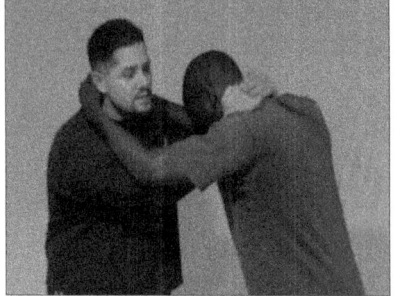

10. He moves his left arm inside his opponent's arm.

11. Once he establishes the inside position, he simulates a head butt.

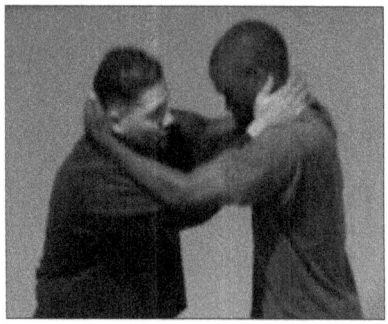

12. And the drill continues…

TARGET AREAS & TECHNIQUES

RAKING

The eye rake is another effective clinch fighting technique that can produce devastating results. There are two types of eye rakes that you have at your disposal from the inside position. They include:

Thumb - This type of eye rake is delivered with a quick swipe of the thumb across the assailant's eyes. Be certain not to confuse the eye rake with its cousin, the single thumb gouge that penetrates deep into the eye socket.

Fingers - This type of eye rake is delivered with all four of your fingers (thumb excluded, of course) in either a downward or horizontal raking motion.

When delivering eye rakes, be certain to resume the neck clamp position after you've successfully delivered the strike.

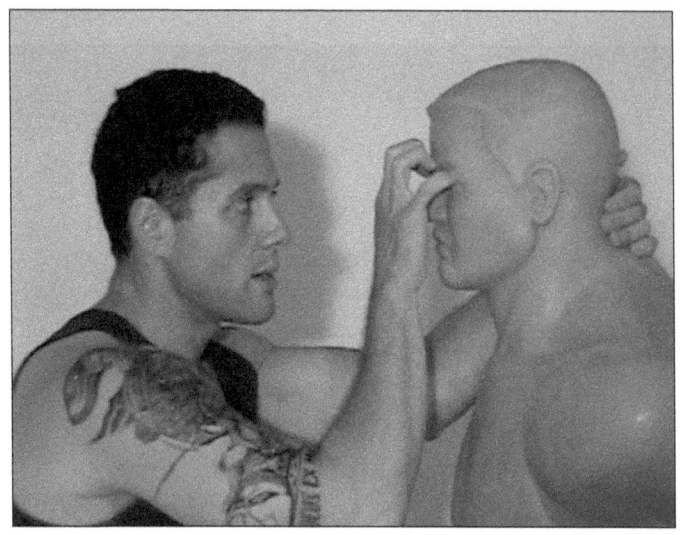

Pictured here, the finger rake.

Pictured here, the thumb rake.

TARGET AREAS & TECHNIQUES

THUMB RAKE DRILL

In this training exercise, we're going to integrate the thumb rake with the swimming drill.

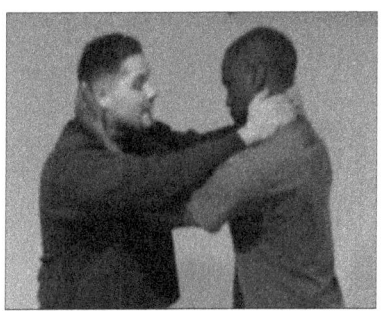

1. Franco starts the drill from the outside position.

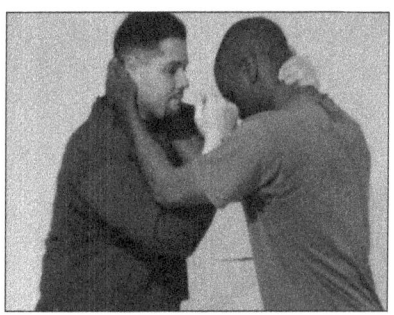

2. Next, he swims his right arm inside the opponent's arm.

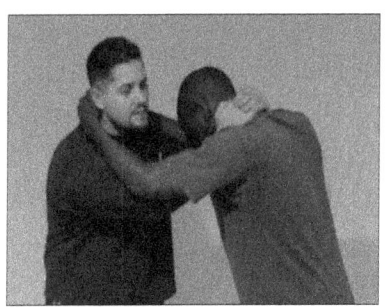

3. He moves his left arm inside his opponent's arm.

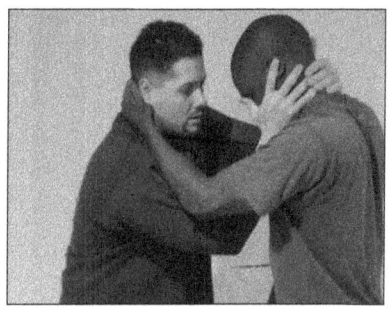

4. From the inside position, he simulates a thumb rake.

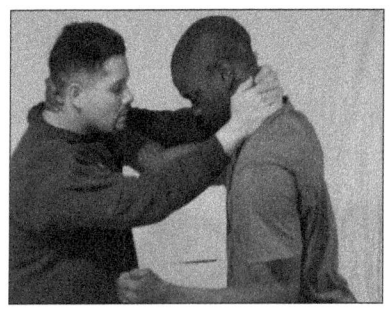

5. Franco's partner begins the swimming drill.

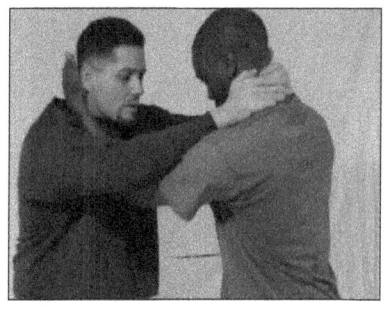

6. He swims his left arm inside Franco's arm.

ENGAGE WITH RAGE

7. Next, he swims his right arm inside Franco's arm.

8. From the inside position, he simulates a thumb rake.

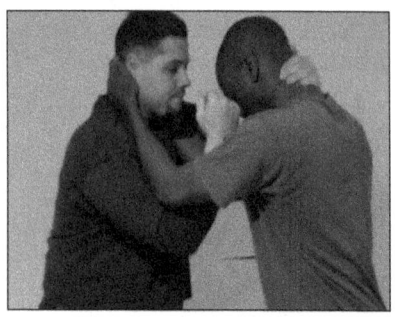
9. Franco swims his right arm inside the opponent's arm.

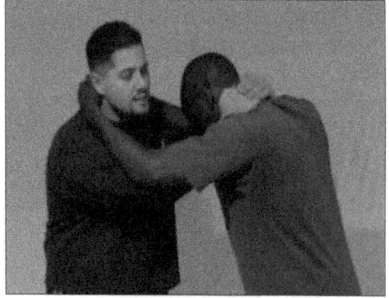
10. He moves his left arm inside his opponent's arm.

11. Once he establishes the inside position, he simulates a head butt.

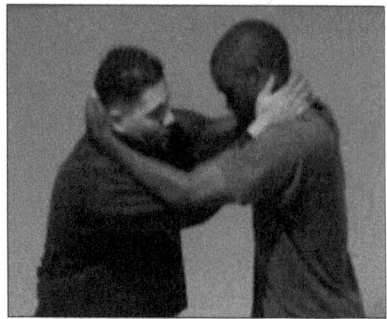
12. And the cycle continues…

TARGET AREAS & TECHNIQUES

THUMB RAKE & HEAD BUTT DRILL

Here, we're going to integrate both the thumb rake and head butt with the swimming drill.

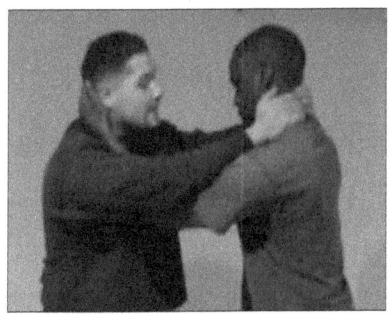

1. Franco starts the drill from the outside position.

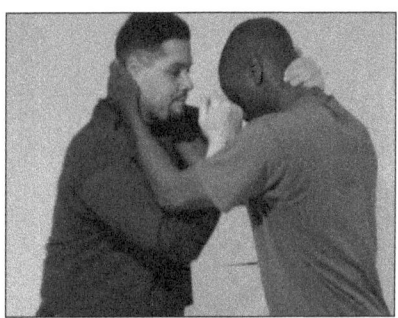

2. He swims his right arm inside the opponent's arm.

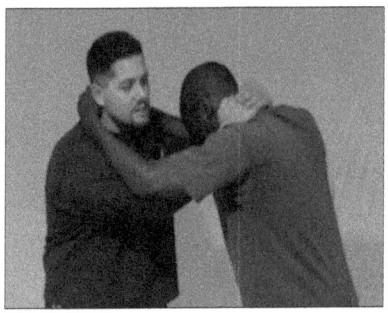

3. He moves his left arm inside his opponent's arm.

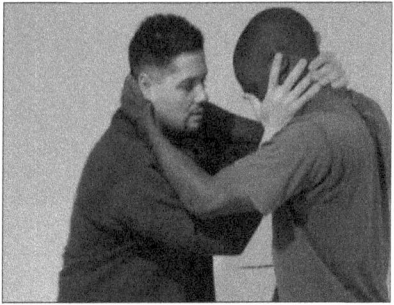

4. From the inside position, he simulates a thumb rake.

5. Followed by a simulated head butt strike.

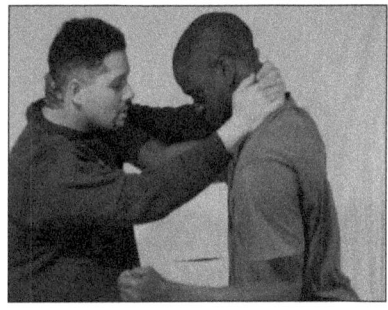

6. Next, Franco's partner begins the swimming drill.

ENGAGE WITH RAGE

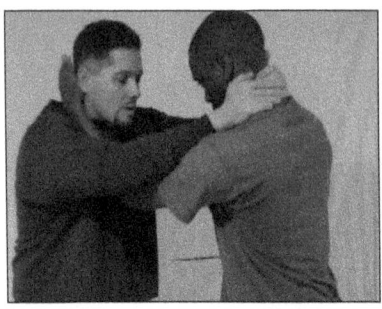
7. He swims his left arm inside Franco's arm.

8. Next, he swims his right arm inside Franco's arm.

8. From the inside position, he simulates a thumb rake.

8. Followed by a head butt strike.

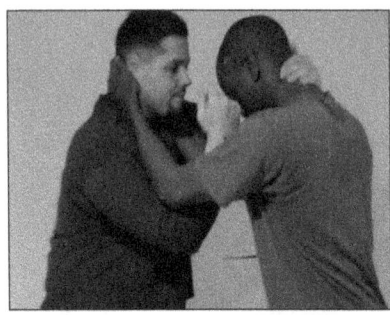
9. Next, Franco swims his right arm inside the opponent's arm.

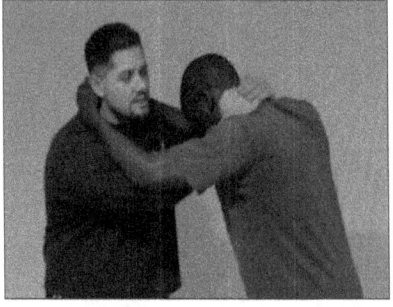
10. He moves his left arm inside his opponent's arm and the drill continues...

TARGET AREAS & TECHNIQUES

SOLO THUMB RAKE & HEAD BUTT DRILL

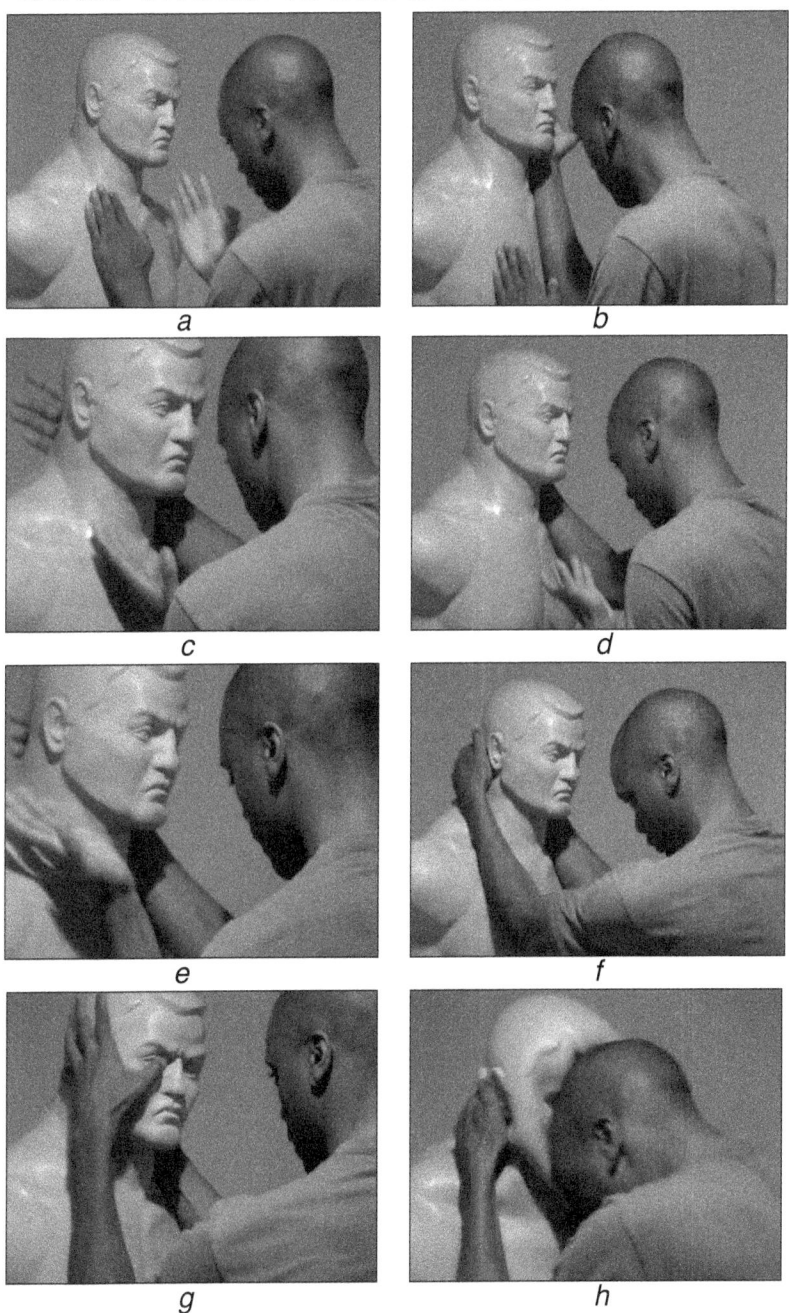

GOUGING

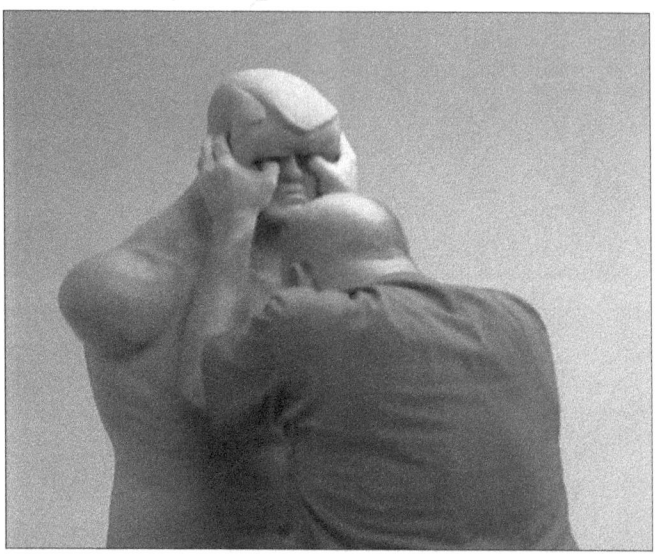

Gouging the eyes can produce devastating results inside the clinch, and it can be delivered when either one or two hands.

To perform the gouge, place one hand on each side of the assailant's face. Stabilize your hands by wrapping your fingers around both sides of your assailant's jaw. Immediately drive both your thumbs into the assailant's eye sockets. Maintain and increase forceful pressure.

The double-thumb gouge can cause temporary or permanent blindness, shock, and unconsciousness.

WARNING: The double-thumb gouge should only be used in life-and-death situations! Be certain that it is legally warranted and justified.

TARGET AREAS & TECHNIQUES

BITING

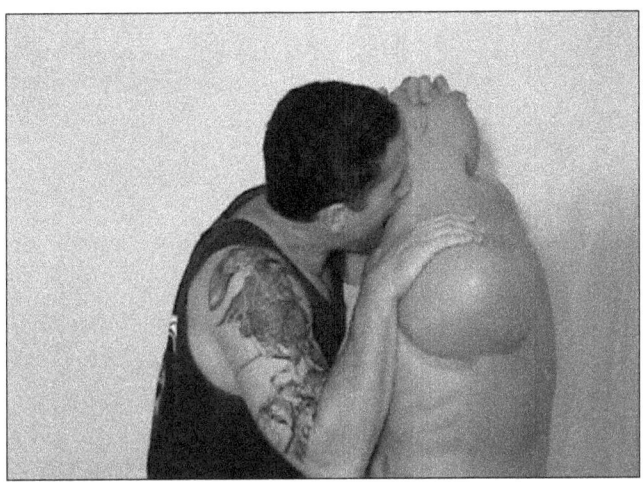

When engaged in the clinch, you can use your teeth for biting the assailant's nose, ears, and throat. Although a deep, penetrating bite is extremely painful, it also transmits a powerful psychological message to your assailant. It lets him know that you are willing to do anything to survive.

CAUTION: Biting should only be used in a do-or-die situation; you run the risk of contracting communicable diseases.

PALM JOLT

The palm jolt is a quick and powerful, open-hand blow that can be delivered from either hand. Contact is made with the heel of your palm with the fingers pointing up. Targets include your assailant's nose and chin.

Unlike the palm-heel strike, this technique is delivered in close-quarters, so it doesn't require you to torque your shoulder, hips, and foot into the direction of the strike. Power comes from the upward force of the elbows and shoulder.

TARGET AREAS & TECHNIQUES

HAMMER FIST

The hammer fist (short arc) is a quick and powerful strike delivered at close range to the adversary. Your target is the assailant's nose.

To deliver the hammer fist, begin by raising your fist with your elbow flexed. Quickly whip your clenched fist down in a vertical line onto the bridge of your assailant's nose. Remember to keep your elbow bent on impact and maintain your balance throughout execution.

ELBOW STRIKES

Elbows strikes are devastating in close-quarter combat. They're explosive, deceptive, and difficult to stop. For the purposes of clinch fighting, elbow strikes should be delivered vertically, and in some cases, horizontally.

Vertical Elbow - The vertical elbow strike travels vertically to the assailant's face or throat. It can be executed from either the right or left side of the body.

To perform the strike, raise your elbow vertically (with the elbow flexed) until your hand is next to the side of your head. The striking surface is the point of the elbow. The power for this strike is acquired through the quick extension of the legs at the moment of impact.

Horizontal Elbow - The horizontal elbow strike travels horizontally to the assailant's face or throat. It can also be executed from either the right or left side of the body.

To perform the strike, rotate your hips and shoulders horizontally into your target. The striking surface is the elbow point.

TARGET AREAS & TECHNIQUES

ELBOW SWIMMING DRILL

In this training exercise, we're going to integrate the vertical elbow strike with the swimming drill.

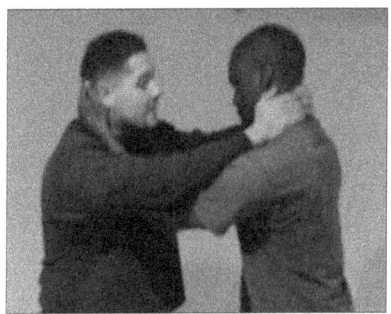

1. Franco starts the drill from the outside position.

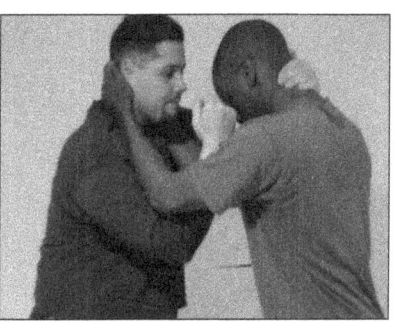

2. He swims his right arm inside the opponent's arm.

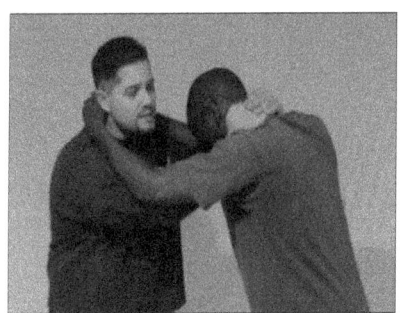

3. Next, he moves his left arm inside his opponent's arm.

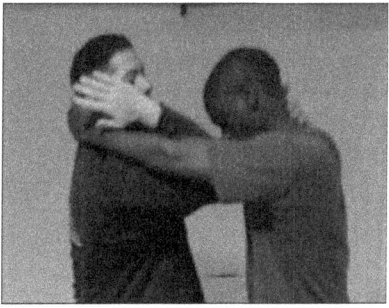

4. From the inside position, he simulates a vertical elbow strike.

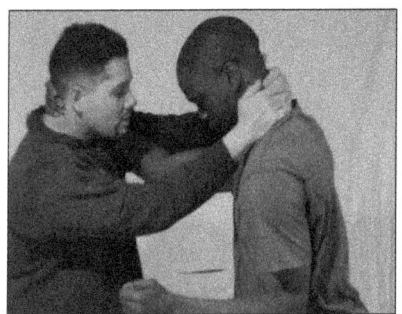

5. Franco's partner begins the swimming drill.

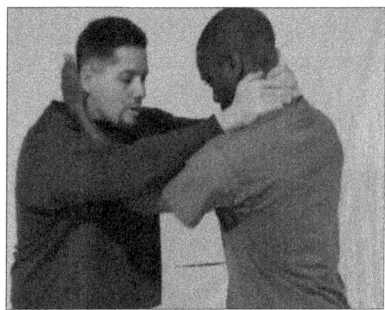

6. He swims his left arm inside Franco's arm.

ENGAGE WITH RAGE

7. Next, he swims his right arm inside Franco's arm.

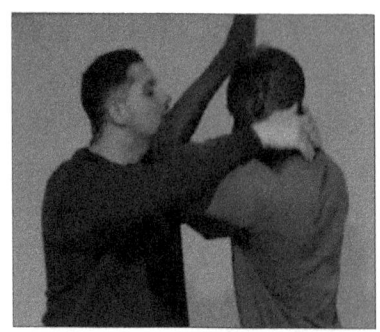

8. From the inside position, he simulates a vertical elbow strike.

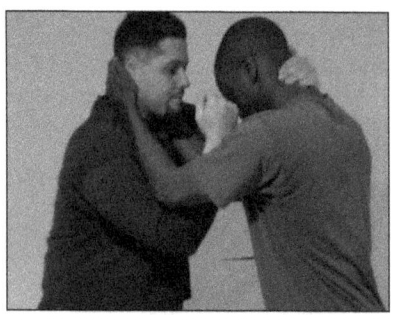

9. Franco swims his right arm inside the opponent's arm.

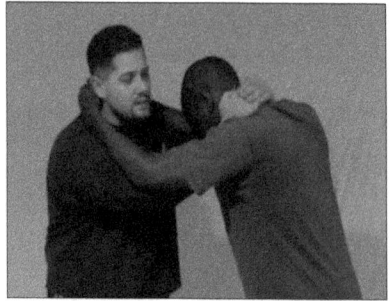

10. He moves his left arm inside his opponent's arm.

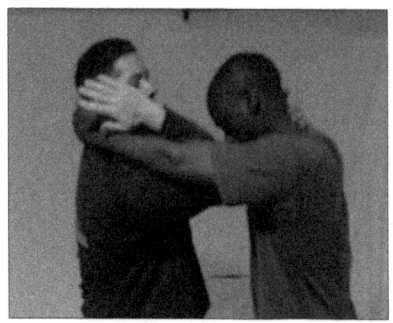

11. Once he establishes the inside position, he simulates a another vertical elbow strike.

12. And the drill continues...

TARGET AREAS & TECHNIQUES

ELBOW FOCUS MITT DRILL

Step 1: In this training exercise, we're going to deliver powerful vertical elbow strikes on the focus mitts. Notice how the striker (left) places his left hand on Franco's neck.

Step 2: As the striker prepares to deliver the strike, Franco holds the focus mitt at the side of his head. Caution: Be certain your training partner has mastered accuracy with this elbow strike before holding it close to your head.

Step 3: While maintaining contact with Franco's neck, the striker delivers a devastating vertical elbow at the focus mitt.

Step 4: The striker returns to the starting position, ready to deliver another strike.

A good workout would consist of delivering 100 elbow strikes from each arm. Depending on your level of conditioning, your mileage may vary.

SHAVING FOREARM

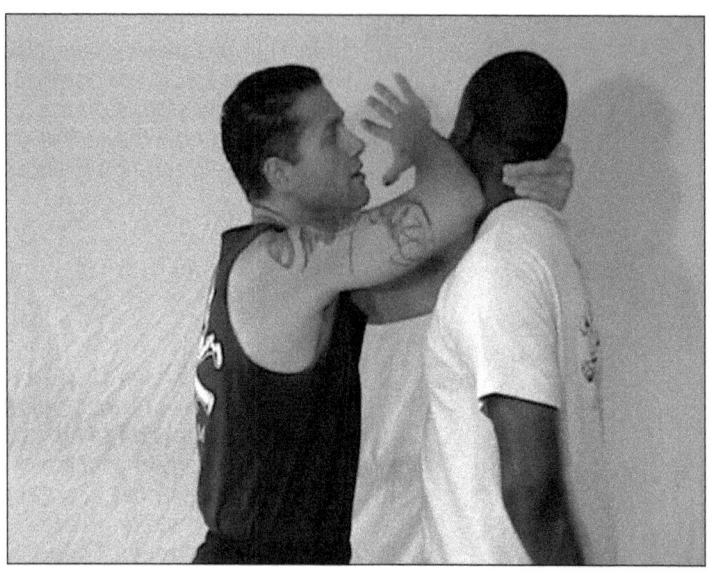

Unlike the classic elbow strike, the shaving forearm is not an actual impact technique. Rather, it grinds against sensitive facial targets (think in terms of a rolling pin), causing excruciating pain for the adversary. This unorthodox technique can be delivered horizontally, vertically and diagonally to the assailant's face.

TARGET AREAS & TECHNIQUES

BICEP POP

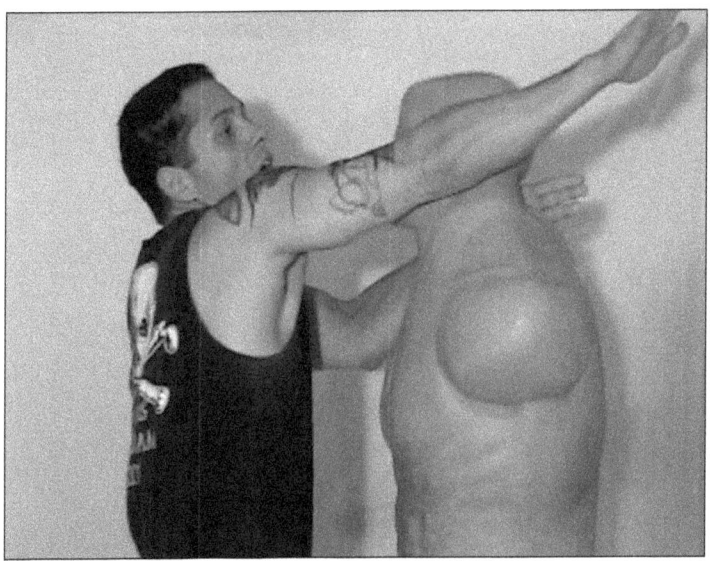

The bicep pop is a counter-measure technique used when your adversary tucks his head into your chest to avoid being hit. Essentially, it's a quick and powerful snap of your arm (biceps region), that forces his head back, allowing you to resume your offensive attack.

KNEE STRIKES

The knee strike is another devastating clinch fighting strike that can drop a formidable assailant to the ground. Depending on how the adversary is standing, the knee strike can be delivered vertically and diagonally, and you can attack either his groin or thighs (both front and lateral).

When delivering the knee strike, be certain to make contact with your patella and not your lower thigh. To guarantee sufficient power, <u>deliver all your knee strikes with your rear leg</u>.

TARGET AREAS & TECHNIQUES

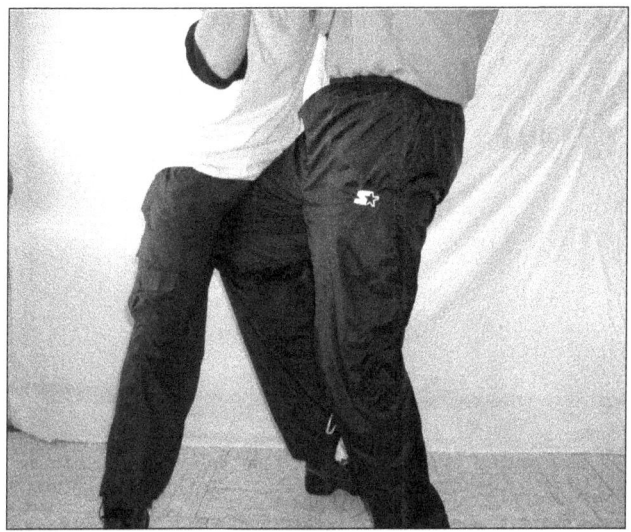

When delivering the vertical knee strike, keep your rear leg bent with your toes pointed to the ground. This toe position helps maintain proper skeletal alignment, promotes muscular relaxation, protects your toes from injury, and facilitates rapid delivery.

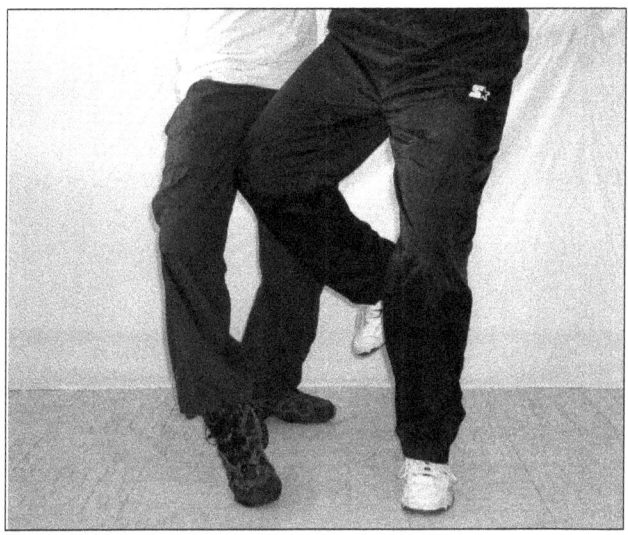

The rear diagonal knee strike travels on a diagonal plane to the assailant's thigh or groin.

KNEE SWIMMING DRILL

In this training exercise, we're going to integrate the vertical knee strike with the swimming drill.

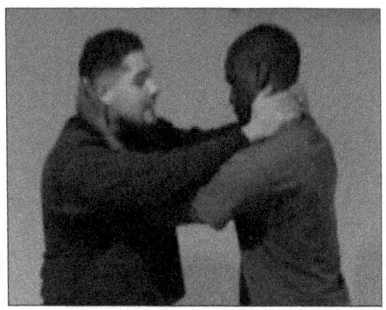

1. Franco starts the drill from the outside position.

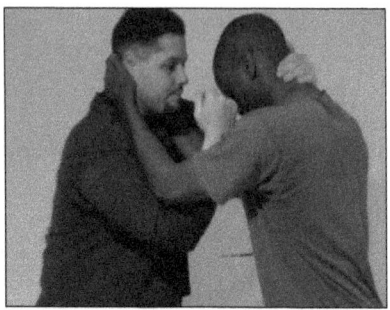

2. He swims his right arm inside the opponent's arm.

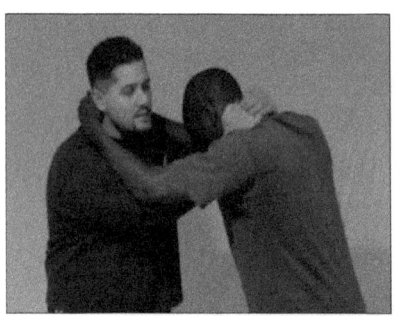

3. Next, he moves his left arm inside his opponent's arm.

4. From the inside position, he simulates a knee strike.

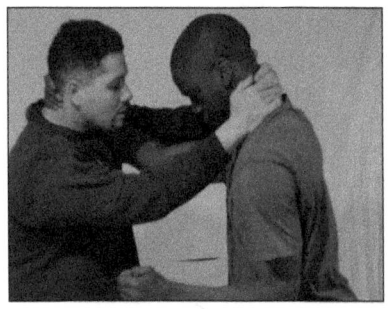

5. Franco's partner begins the swimming drill.

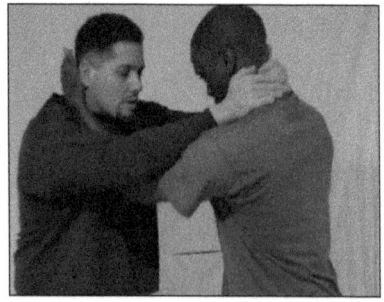

6. He swims his left arm inside Franco's arm.

TARGET AREAS & TECHNIQUES

7. Next, he swims his right arm inside Franco's arm.

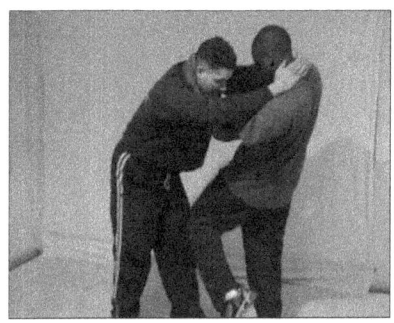

8. From the inside position, he simulates a vertical knee strike.

9. Franco swims his right arm inside the opponent's arm.

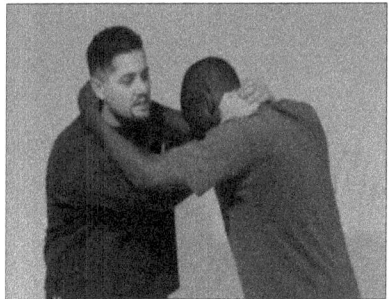

10. He moves his left arm inside his opponent's arm.

11. Once he establishes the inside position, he simulates a head butt.

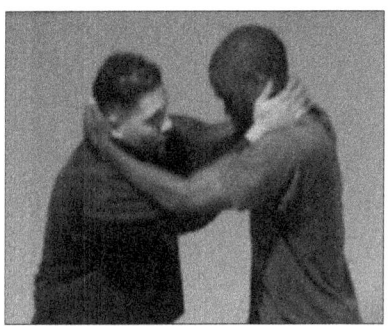

12. And the cycle continues...

ENGAGE WITH RAGE

KNEE FOCUS MITT DRILL

Step 1: In this training exercise, we're going to deliver vertical knee strikes on the focus mitts. Notice how the striker (left) places both hands on Franco's neck.

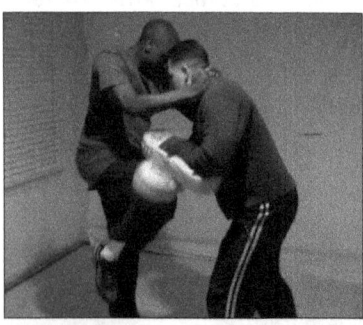

Step 2: While maintaining control of Franco's neck, the striker delivers a powerful knee strike.

Step 3: The striker returns to the starting position, ready to deliver another strike.

Step 4: Next, he delivers another knee strike.

A good workout would consist of delivering 50-75 knee strikes from each leg.

TARGET AREAS & TECHNIQUES

NECK CRANK

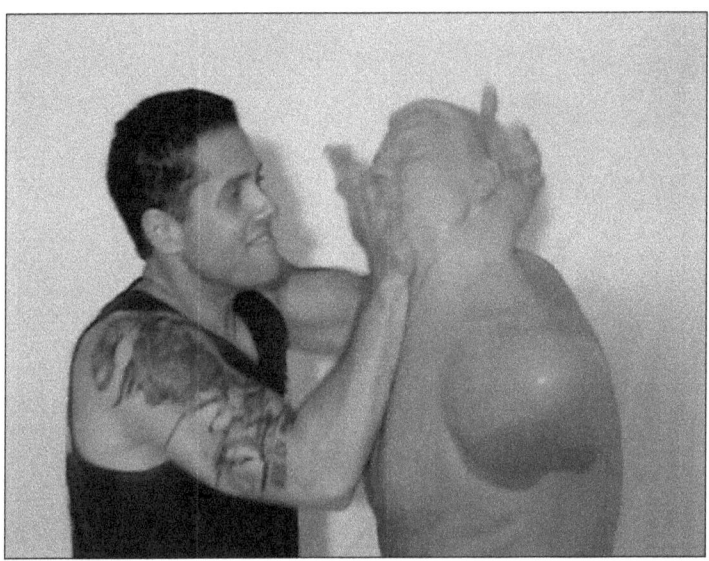

The neck crank is generally used at the completion of your offensive assault inside of the clinch. It's also used to set up a possible "finishing hold", such as a standing rear naked choke.

To apply the neck crank, place your right palm under the opponent's chin, and your left hand against the back of the opponent's head.

Next, simultaneously twist the opponent's head diagonally upwards in a counter clockwise direction. When done correctly, the opponent's entire body will turn, exposing his back to a finishing choke hold.

Warning! Be very careful with this technique as it can cause severe injury to the opponent's neck and cervical vertebrae.

FINISHING CHOKES

There are a couple chokes that can be applied directly after the neck crank. However, one of the most effective chokes you can employ is the rear naked choke, which will put your adversary to sleep within a matter of seconds.

To apply the naked choke effectively, follow these important steps: (1) be certain to apply the choke from behind your assailant, (2) begin the naked choke by positioning your right arm around your assailant's neck with your palm facing down, (3) make certain the assailant's windpipe is positioned in the crook of your right elbow, (4) put your right hand on your left shoulder, (5) place the blade side of your left forearm on the back of the assailant's neck, and (6) with your right arm, slowly squeeze the lateral sides of the assailant's neck.

TARGET AREAS & TECHNIQUES

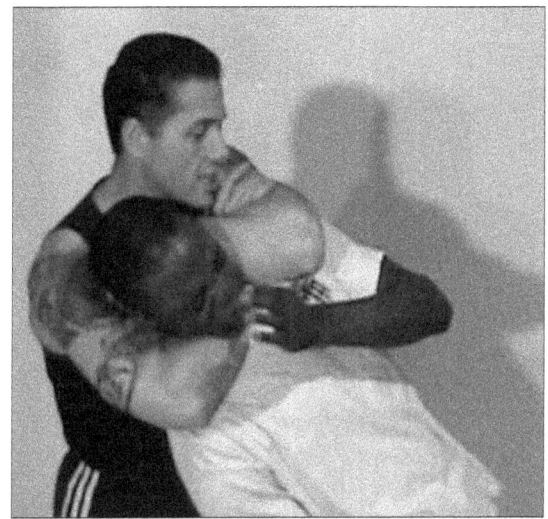

Pictured here, a brutal variation of the rear naked choke. This wicked technique requires you to apply your forearm against the assailant's windpipe. Warning! This technique can be deadly and must only be used in self-defense situations that warrant the application of deadly force.

The following photos demonstrate the neck crank technique integrated with the rear naked choke.

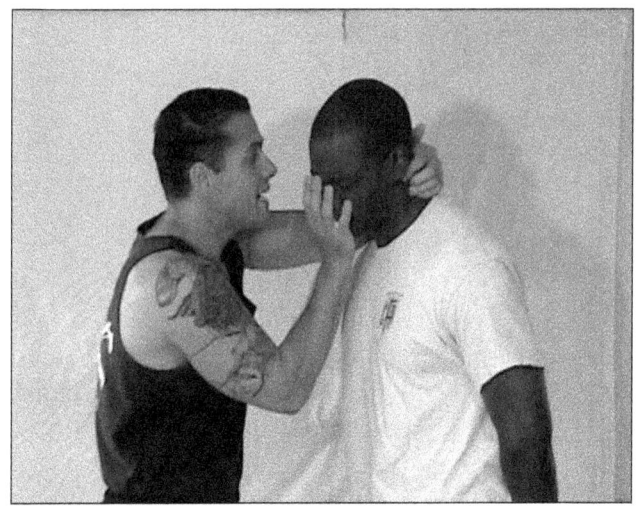

Step 1: Franco sets up the neck crank.

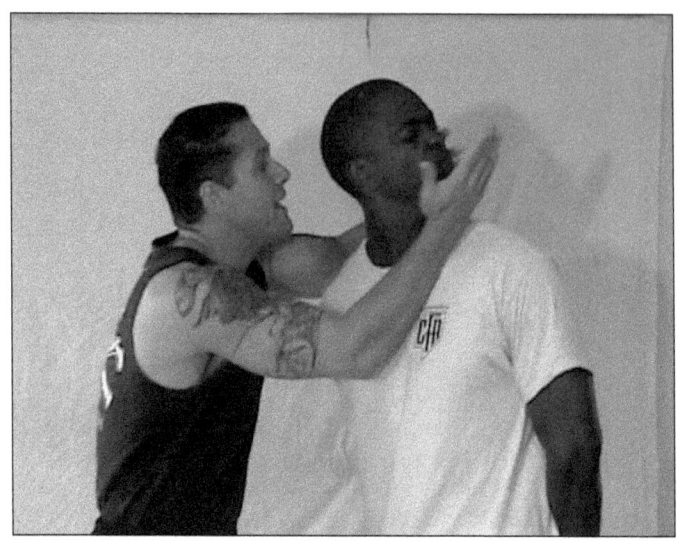

Step 2: Next, he twists his assailant's head diagonally upward.

Step 3: As the adversary turns his back, Franco seamlessly applies a rear naked choke.

TARGET AREAS & TECHNIQUES

NECK CRANK SWIMMING DRILL

In this training exercise, we're going to integrate both the neck crank and rear naked choke with the swimming drill.

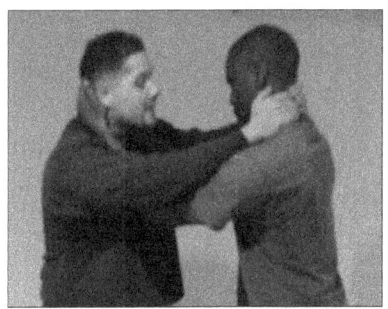

1. Franco starts the drill from the outside position.

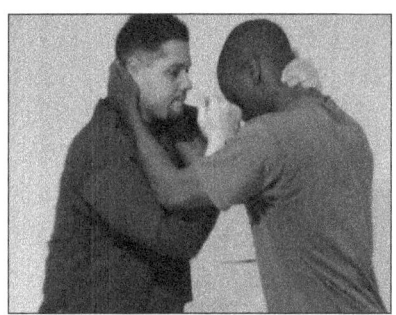

2. He slides his right arm inside the opponent's arm.

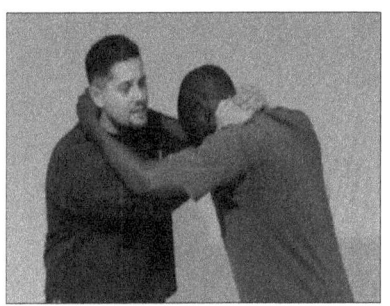

3. Next, he moves his left arm inside his opponent's arm.

4. From the inside position, Franco begins the neck crank.

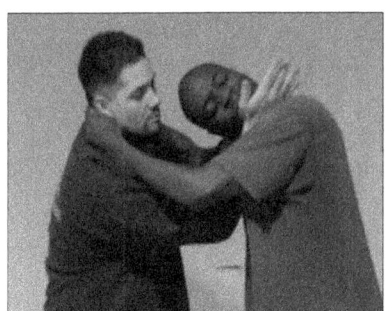

5. Franco continues with the neck crank.

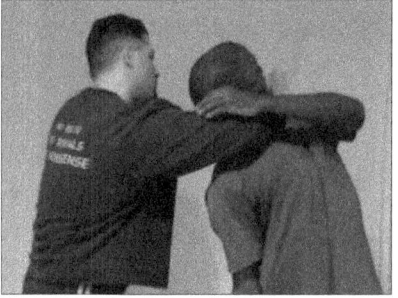

6. He slides his right arm under his training partner's chin.

ENGAGE WITH RAGE

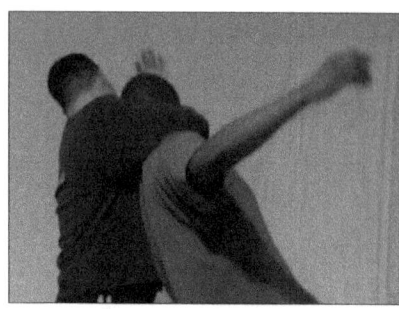 

7. Franco begins to apply the rear naked choke.

8. The drill is complete once Franco solidifies the choke hold.

CHAPTER FIVE
Extreme Clinch Fighting

ENGAGE WITH RAGE

EXTREME CLINCH FIGHTING

ADVANCED TECHNIQUES

In the previous chapters, I've addressed conventional clinch fighting techniques that can be readily applied in an emergency self-defense situation. However, this chapter is going to introduce you to the most vicious form of clinch combat known to man… **Razing!**

In my Widow Maker Program, *Razing* is defined as a series of vicious close quarter techniques designed to physically and psychologically extirpate a criminal attacker.

These close quarter techniques are executed at various beats: (i.e., half beat, quarter beat and zero beat) and they include the following:

- Eye raking
- Tearing
- Biting
- Elbow strikes
- Head butts
- Bicep pops
- Finishing chokes

- Eye gouging
- Crushing
- Hair pulling
- Shaving forearms
- Hair Pulling
- Neck cranks

ENGAGE WITH RAGE

Razing is the most devastating form of unarmed fighting. Its brutal and invasive characteristics are both physically and psychologically traumatic for the recipient.

The overwhelming nature of razing invokes instantaneous panic by delivering a destructiveness exceeding that of a deadly and evil criminal aggressor. When razing is properly performed, it accomplishes the following objectives during a clinch fight:

1. Cognitive Brain Shutdown - The brutal and overwhelming nature of razing overrides the opponent's cognitive brain preventing him from any lucid thought process. Since razing is so fast and ferocious, the opponent's cognitive brain can't process what is actually happening to him.

2. Instant Damage - Razing is simply indefensible! The speed and proximity at which these quarter beat hits are delivered is truly overwhelming. The bottom line is, they're just too fast and too close for the opponent to react defensively. In many ways, razing is likened to an angry swarm of wasps, your only hope is to try and escape from the pain.

Finally, because of its devastating power, razing should only be used in a do-or-die self-defense situation that warrants the application of deadly force.

More Advantages of Razing

There are other advantages to adding my razing methodology to your current self-defense regimen. What follows is a brief list:

1. It's unconventional - Razing is a very unusual and unorthodox form of fighting. Even the most seasoned martial artist or street fighter has never been exposed to this unconventional style of combat. As a result, they're unprepared physically and psychologically.

2. Low maintenance - Razing techniques are exceptionally efficient and easy to perform under the duress of real world combat conditions. Unlike kicking and punching, you don't need to spend countless hours perfecting fine motor skill body mechanics.

3. Less chance of injuries - Unlike fisted blows, you don't run the risk of spraining or breaking your wrists or fingers when performing razing techniques.

To the uninitiated, razing will appear bizarre, haphazard, and chaotic. Some might erroneously assume it's a gross motor skill method of fighting. However, nothing can be farther from the truth. Razing is a close-quarter fighting method that requires technical precision, timing, and strategic implementation. Razing is also a culmination of several advanced techniques that do require training and practice to master.

However, this is not to say that you can't just "wing it" and barrage the opponent with a series of gross motor razing technique. It can be done and, in some cases, improvising razing will yield results. However, to really unleash the sheer devastating power of razing, you must learn to deliver it in a tactical and calculated manner.

Best of all, razing is straightforward and can easily be integrated into any style of fighting.

When Can I Apply Razing?

I'd be remiss if I didn't give you a few caveats about razing. First, because of its devastating power, razing should only be used in self-defense situations that warrant the application of deadly force.

Understanding Deadly Force

So what is *deadly force*? First, let me state that you must never use force against anyone unless it is absolutely necessary. Next, "force" is broken down into two levels: deadly and non deadly. Deadly force is defined as violent action known to  create a substantial risk of causing death or serious bodily harm. A person may use deadly force in self-defense only if retaliating against another's deadly force. Non deadly force is an amount of force that does not result in serious bodily injury or death.

Let me be clear, razing can produce serious bodily harm and possible death. They are classified as deadly force techniques and must only be used to protect yourself or a loved one from immediate risk of unlawful deadly criminal attack. Remember, the decision to use deadly force must always be a last resort; after all other means of avoiding violence has been thoroughly exhausted.

Razing should not be used as an intermediate use-of-force tactic. It is not designed to be "toned down" as a compliance tool to gain control over your opponent. It's all or nothing with razing! For it to work effectively, it must be delivered with tremendous force and blistering speed. Frankly, anything less will likely result in the opponent seriously injuring you.

EXTREME CLINCH FIGHTING

Widow Maker's Beat System

In order to truly appreciate the razing method of attack, you need to have a fundamental understanding of my beat system. There are four (4) beat classifications. They include:

• **Full Beat** - your strike has an initiation and retraction phase. Standard punches and blows are generally considered full beat strikes. For example, palm heel, rear cross, etc.)

• **Half Beat** - your strike is delivered through the retraction phase of the previous strike.

• **Quarter Beat** - a rapid series of strikes that never break contact with the target. Quarter beat strikes are primary responsible for creating the psychological panic and trauma for the opponent. While all three beat classifications are important to the Widow Maker program, it's the quarter beat that evokes panic in your adversary.

• **Zero Beat** - full pressure techniques applied to a specific target until it ruptures. Includes gouging, biting and choking techniques. Primary anatomical targets include: the eyes and throat. Zero beat is most often applied at the end of your razing assault.

While there are four unique beat classifications, the razing methodology only uses three. They are: half, quarter and zero beats.

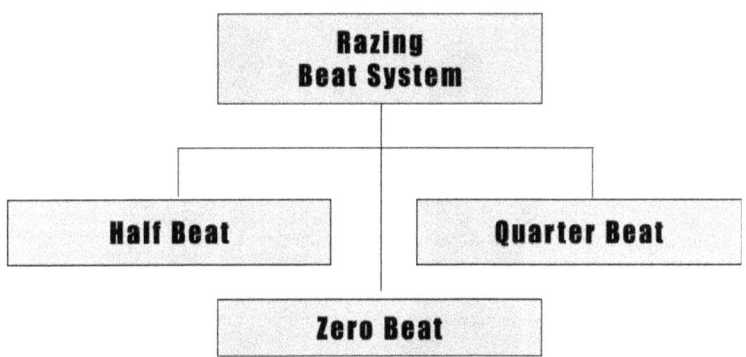

Razing techniques are executed at three different beats.

ENGAGE WITH RAGE

Full Beat Demonstration

Step 1: Franco squares off in a fighting stance.

Step 2: He delivers a punch by extending his arm at his opponent.

Step 3: He retracts his arm back to the starting position.

EXTREME CLINCH FIGHTING

Half Beat Demonstration

Step 1: Franco squares off in a fighting stance.

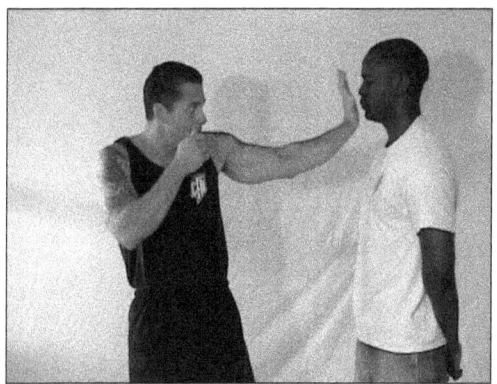

Step 2: He delivers a palm heel strike by extending his arm.

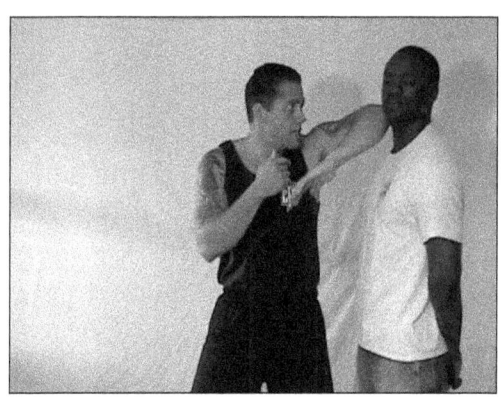

Step 3: As he retracts his arm, he converts it into an elbow strike.

Quarter Beat Demonstration

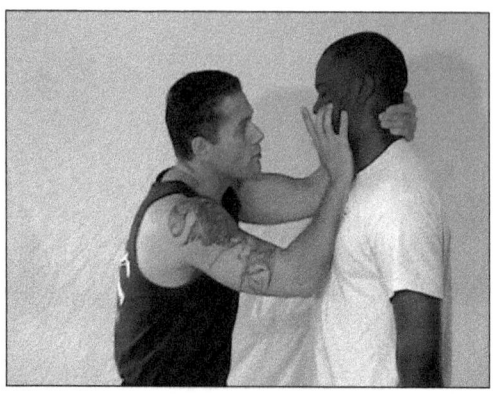

Step 1: Franco begins his quarter beat assault with an eye rake.

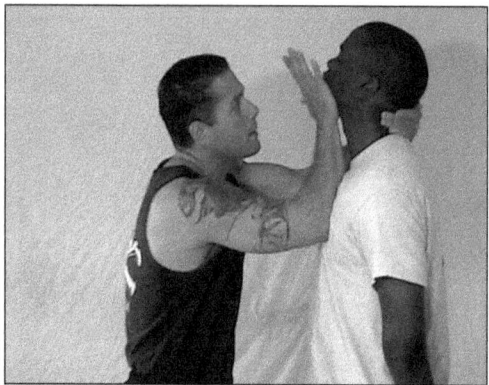

Step 2: Without breaking contact with his opponent's face, he attacks with a palm jolt to the chin.

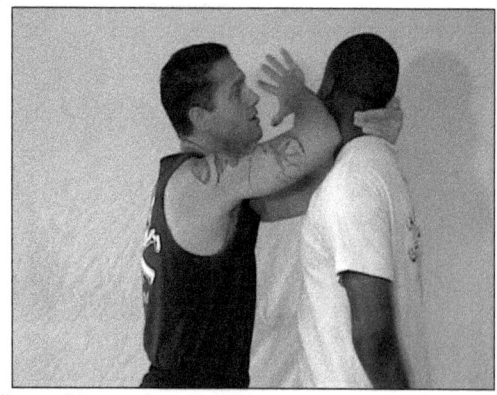

Step 3: Followed by a shaving forearm across his opponent's face.

Zero Beat Demonstration

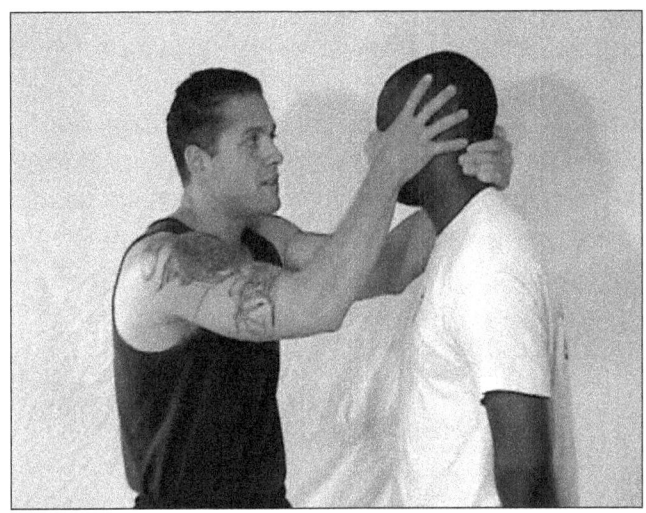

Pictured here, the author demonstrates a zero beat attack... a single thumb gouge.

The rear naked choke is another effective zero beat technique used at the completion phase of razing.

Razing Demonstration

To give you a better understanding of the razing methodology inside the clinch, I've included four different examples. Keep in mind that all of the following razing sequences are performed and completed in just a few seconds. All of these quarter beat techniques should flow naturally, without any predetermined sequence or pattern.

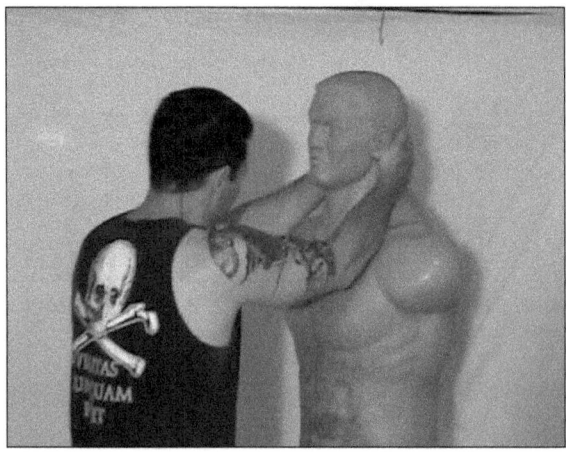

Step 1: Franco begins from the clinch position.

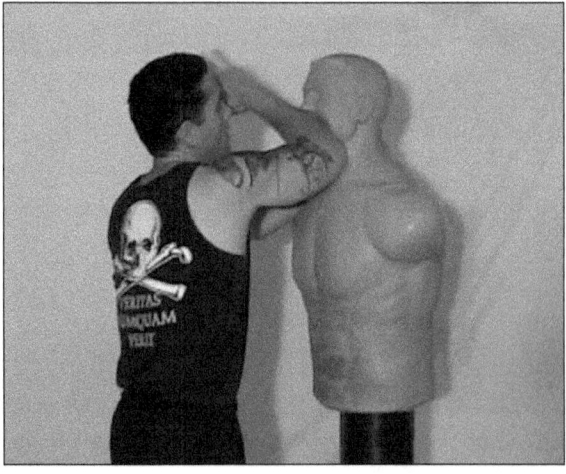

Step 2: The razing begins with a shaving forearm.

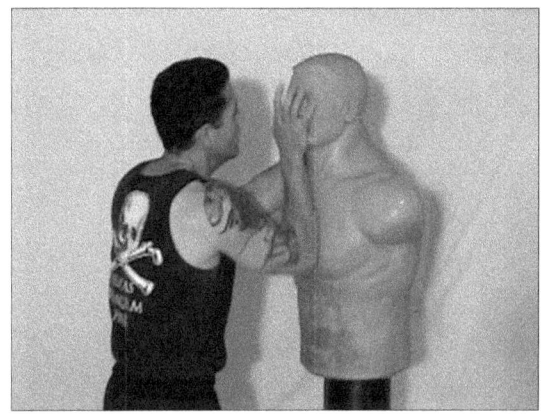
Step 3: Next, he attacks with an eye rake.

Step 4: Followed by a palm jolt.

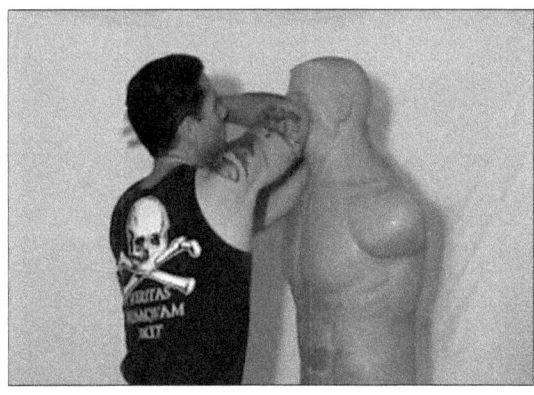
Step 5: Without breaking contact, he delivers a diagonal elbow strike.

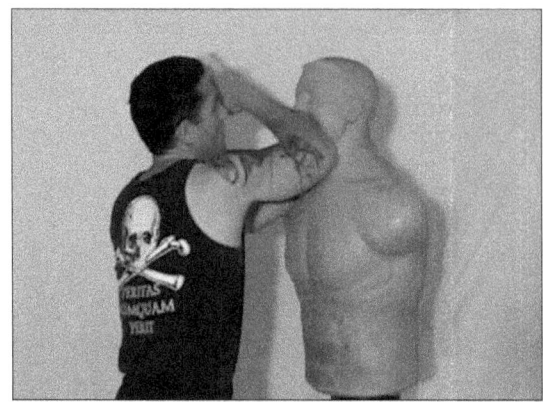
Step 6: Next, he attacks with a reverse shaving forearm.

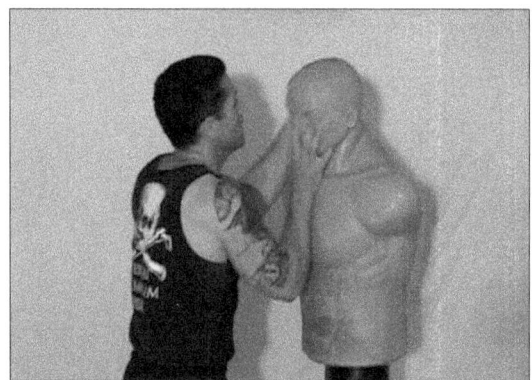
Step 7: The shaving forearm turns into another eye rake attack.

Step 8: Followed by a head butt.

EXTREME CLINCH FIGHTING

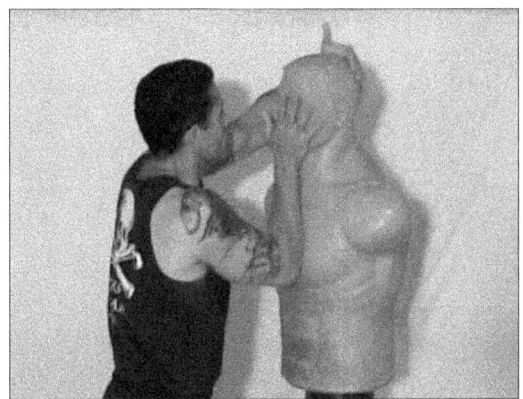

Step 9: Without breaking contact, Franco sets up the neck crank.

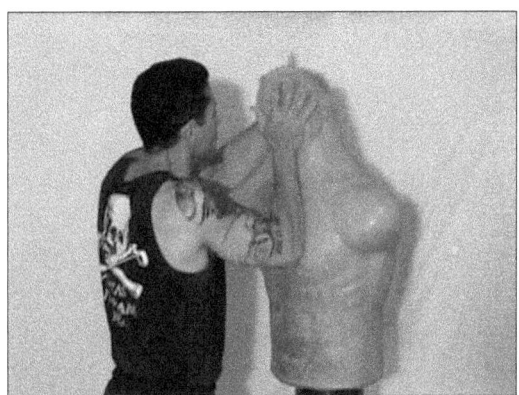

Step 10: He cranks the neck counter clockwise with both hands.

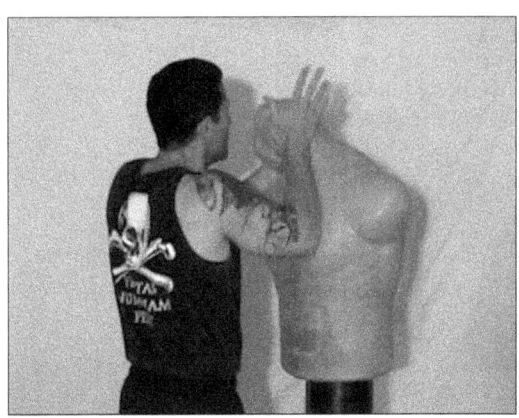

Step 11: The razing sequence is complete.

ENGAGE WITH RAGE

Razing Demonstration #2

Step 1: Franco starts with his left hand anchoring the neck.

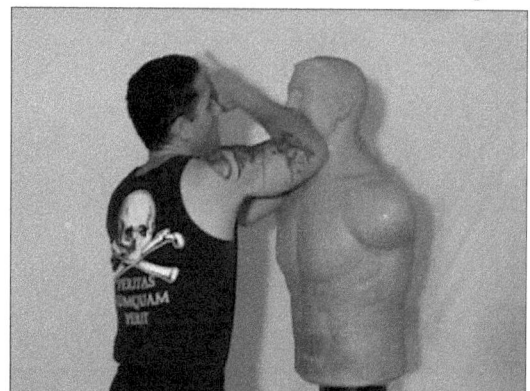

Step 2: The razing begins with a shaving forearm.

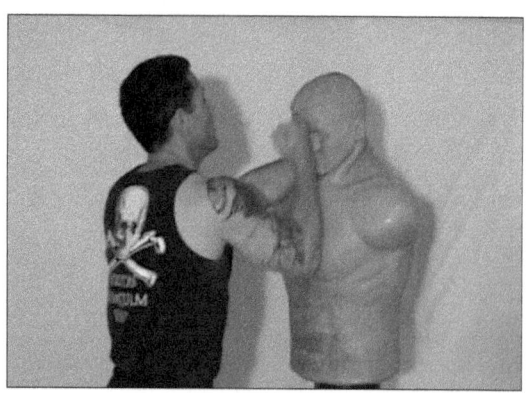

Step 3: Followed by a short arc hammer fist strike to the nose.

EXTREME CLINCH FIGHTING

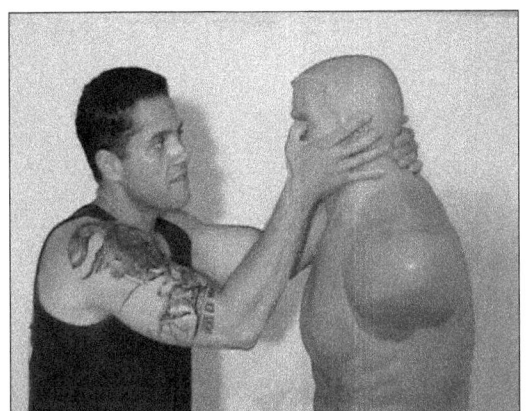

Step 4: Next, he delivers a thumb rake to the eye.

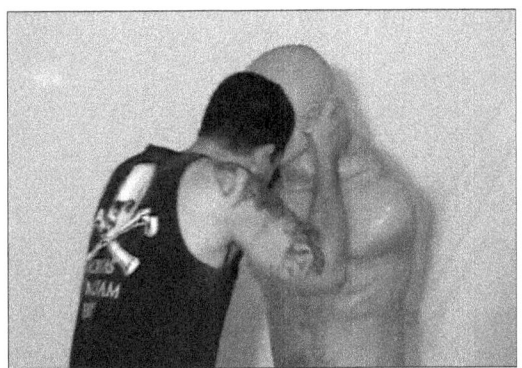

Step 5: Followed by a head butt.

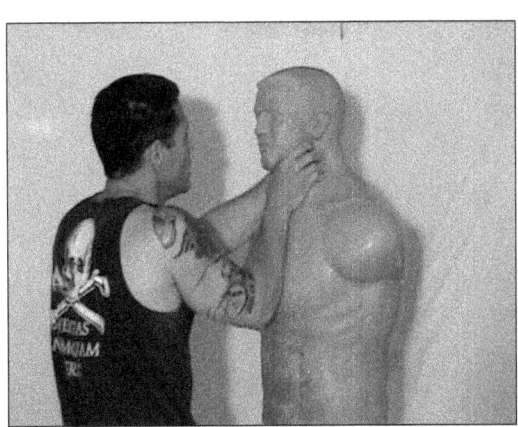

Step 6: The razing sequence is completed with a throat crush.

Razing Demonstration #3

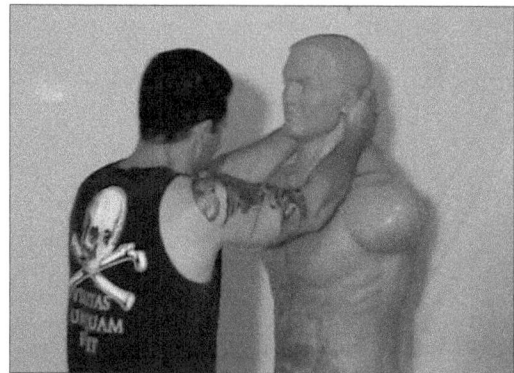

Step 1: Franco starts from the clinch position.

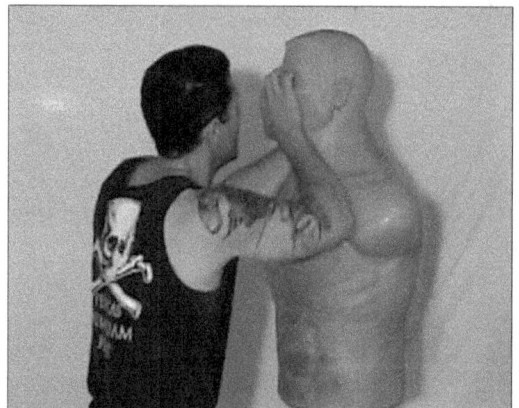

Step 2: The razing begins with an eye rake.

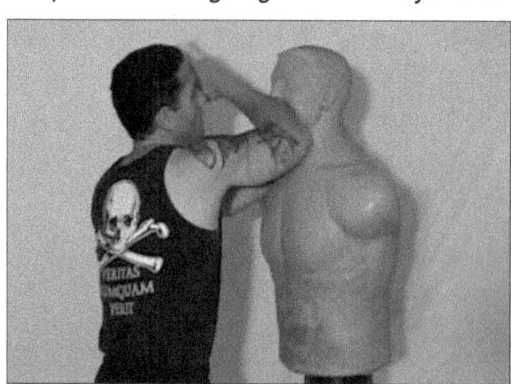

Step 3: Followed by a shaving forearm.

EXTREME CLINCH FIGHTING

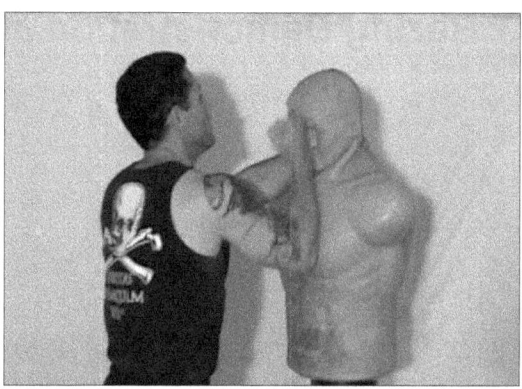

Step 4: Next, a short arc hammer fist strike to the nose.

Step 5: Franco releases the anchor from behind the neck and prepares to deliver a double thumb gouge

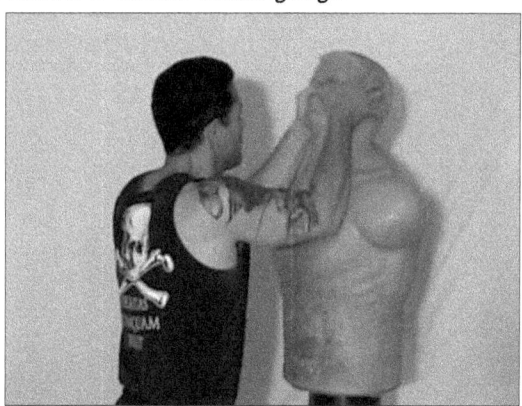

Step 6: The razing sequence ends with a double thumb gouge.

Razing Demonstration #4

Step 1: Franco starts with his left hand anchoring the neck.

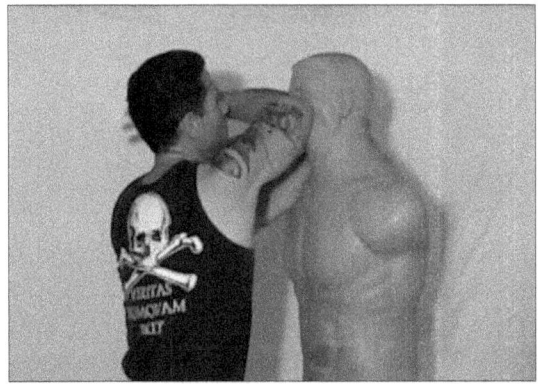

Step 2: He begins with a diagonal elbow strike.

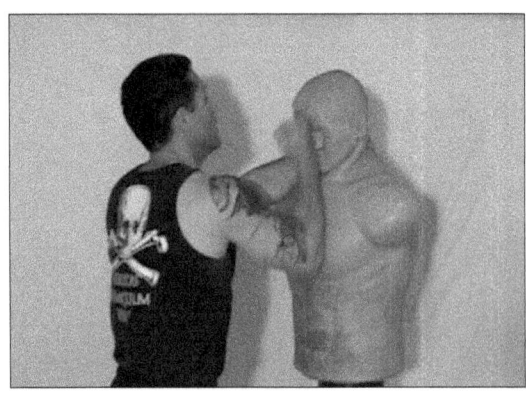

Step 3: Franco follows up with a short arc hammer fist strike.

EXTREME CLINCH FIGHTING

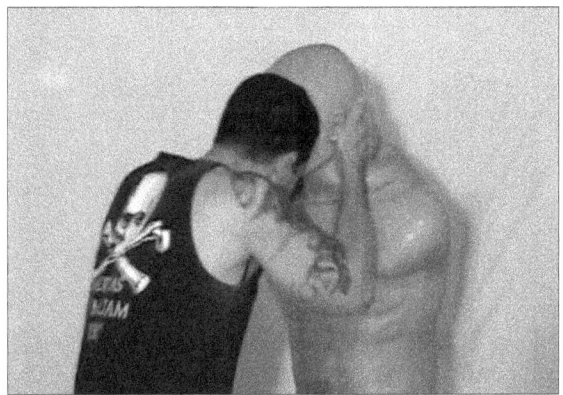

Step 4: Next, a head butt to the nose.

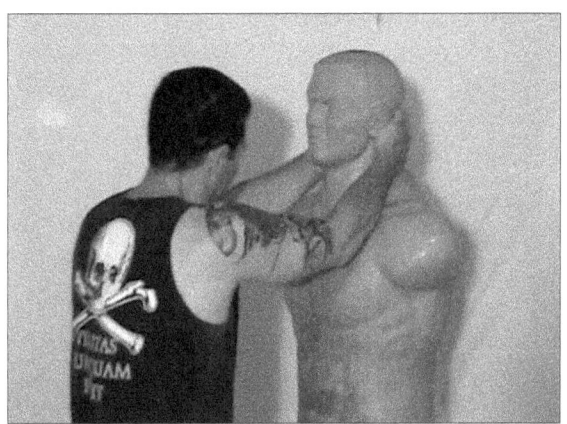

Step 5: He retracts his head, setting up another strike.

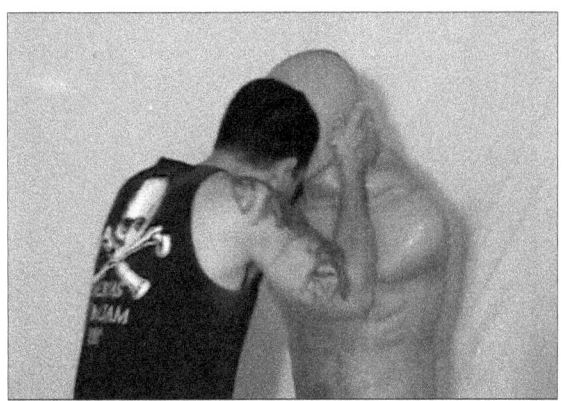

Step 6: He delivers another head butt.

Step 7: Followed by a thumb rake to the eye.

Step 8: Without breaking contact, Franco sets up the neck crank.

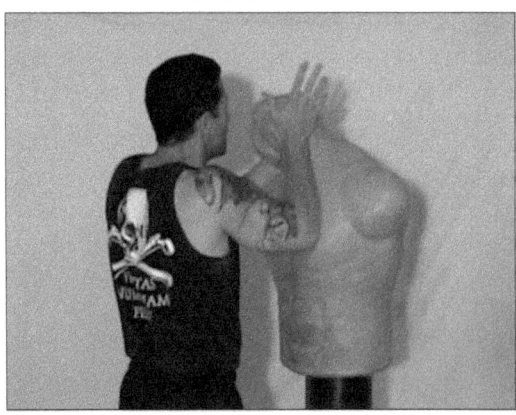
Step 9: The razing sequence is finished with a neck crank.

Razing the Body Opponent Bag

The body opponent bag is, by far, the best piece of training equipment for developing your razing skills and techniques. Unlike the traditional heavy bag, this freestanding mannequin bag provides realistic facial targets that you can attack with full-speed, full-force strikes.

Effective razing skills take time and practice to master. Remember to start out slowly and progressively build up the speed and intensity of your quarter beat strikes. If you're a beginner, avoid the urge to attack the bag with maximum speed and force. Take your time and enjoy the process of learning this invaluable new skill.

What follows is a list of tips to help maximize your razing skills when training on the body opponent bag.

Tips for Razing the Body Opponent Bag

Here are ten important points to keep in mind when razing the body opponent bag.

1. Don't "force the raze". Let your series of strikes flow naturally and easily.

ENGAGE WITH RAGE

2. Don't forget to include biting tactics in your training.

3. Always remain relaxed when razing. Tightening your muscles will only slow you down and break your offensive flow.

4. Get into the habit of executing "zero beat" techniques at the end of your razing combination.

5. Practice your razing skills at least three times per week (30 minutes per workout session) for six consecutive months.

6. Keep your razing movement "clean" and "tight", avoid sloppy telegraphic movements.

7. While the body opponent bag is a useful training tool, understand and recognize its inherent limitations. Remember, razing a stationary mannequin bag is nothing like razing an adrenaline induced human being.

8. If you want to improve the speed and overall flow of your razing techniques during your workout, you can apply petroleum jelly to the BOB's face.

9. Never stand squarely in front of the bag when razing. Not only does this expose vital targets, it also diminishes your balance and inhibits your footwork. Always try to maintain a forty-five degree stance from your assailant.

10. Practice razing with both your weak and dominant hands.

Body Opponent Bag Targets

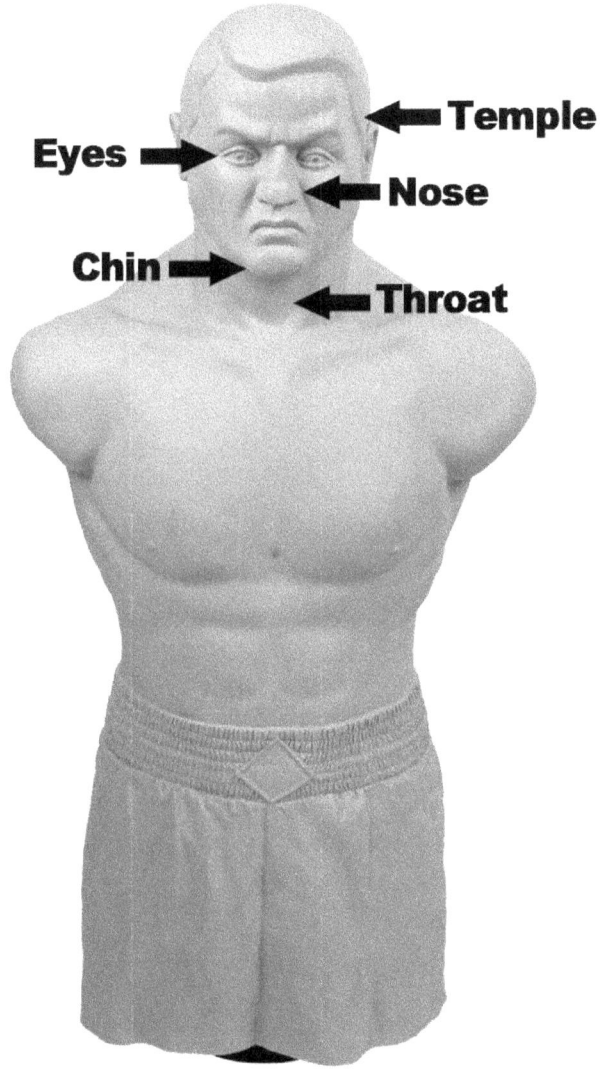

The primary razing targets on the body opponent bag include: the temple, eyes, nose, chin, and throat.

Right Hand Razing Combinations

The following ten razing combinations should be performed with your right hand while anchoring the neck with your left.

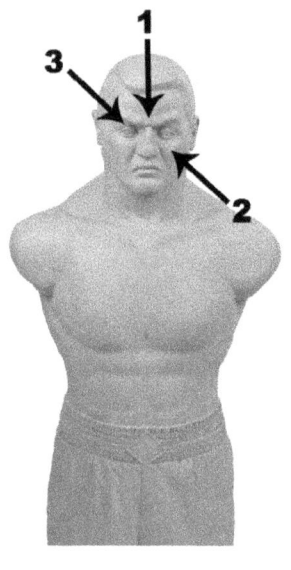

Razing Combination #1

1. Eye Rake
2. Shaving Forearm
3. Hammer Fist Strike

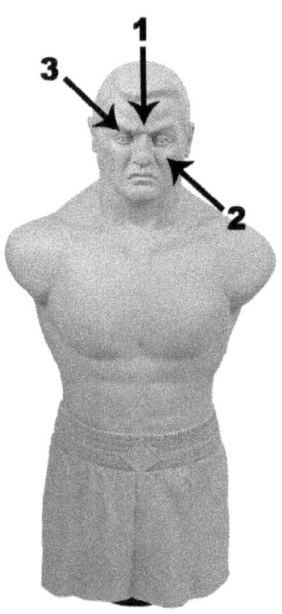

Razing Combination #2

1. Short Arc Hammer Fist
2. Diagonal Elbow
3. Diagonal Eye Rake

EXTREME CLINCH FIGHTING

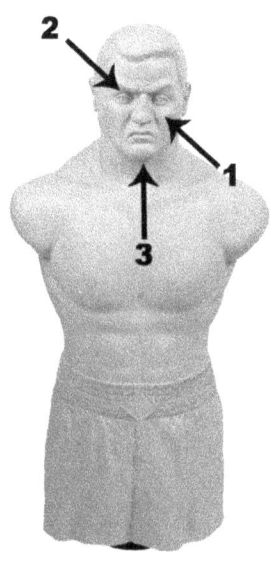

Razing Combination #3

1. Shaving Forearm
2. Reverse Shaving Forearm
3. Palm Jolt

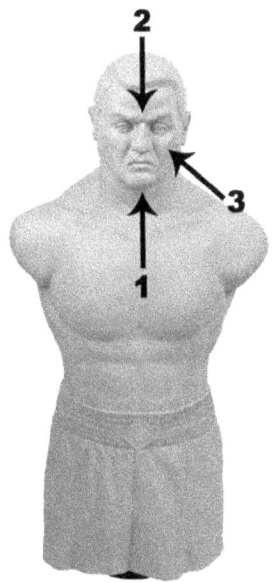

Razing Combination #4

1. Palm Jolt
2. Eye Rake
3. Shaving Forearm

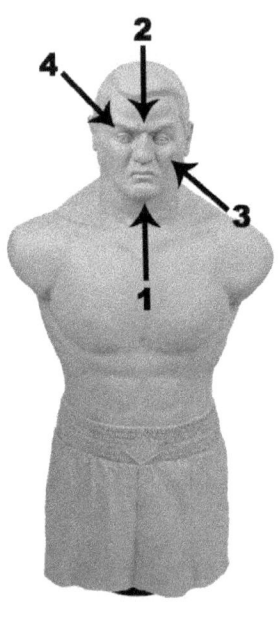

Razing Combination #5

1. Vertical Elbow
2. Short Arc Hammer Fist
3. Shaving Forearm
4. Diagonal Eye Rake

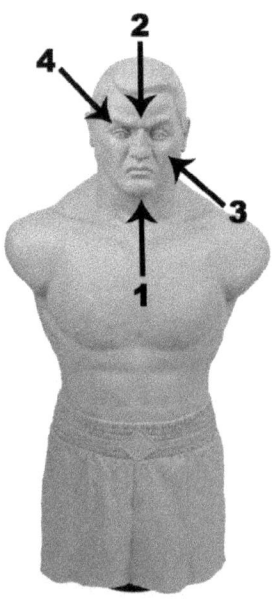

Razing Combination #6

1. Palm Jolt
2. Short Arc Hammer Fist
3. Shaving Forearm
4. Reverse Shaving Forearm

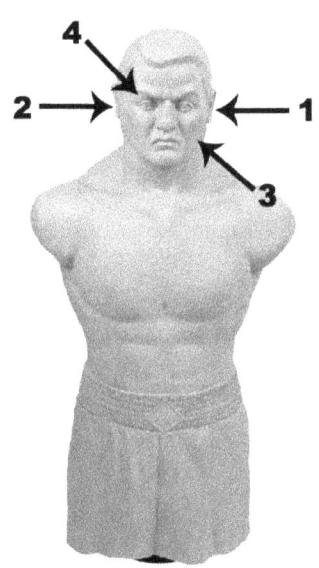

Razing Combination #7

1. Horizontal Elbow
2. Shaving Forearm
3. Shaving Forearm
4. Short Arc Hammer Fist

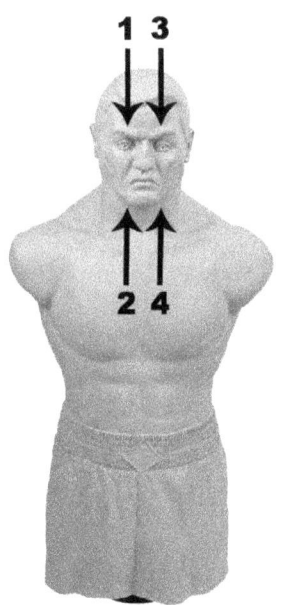

Razing Combination #8

1. Eye Rake
2. Palm Jolt
3. Eye Rake
4. Palm Jolt

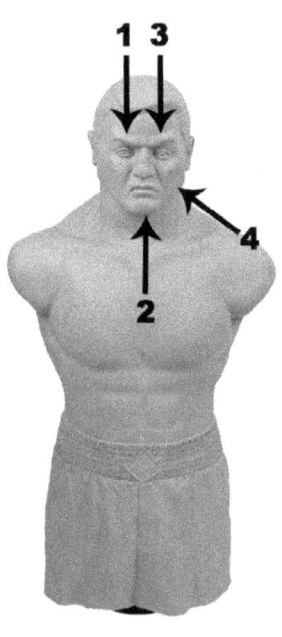

Razing Combination #9

1. Short Arc Hammer Fist
2. Vertical Elbow
3. Eye Rake
4. Shaving Forearm

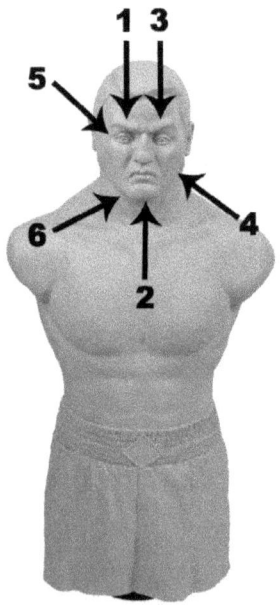

Razing Combination #10

1. Eye Rake
2. Vertical Elbow
3. Short Arc Hammer Fist
4. Shaving Forearm
5. Reverse Shaving Forearm
6. Neck Crank

Razing Limitations

Unfortunately, razing is not the be-all and end-all self-defense solution. Actually, no self-defense technique or methodology is an end in itself. Functional self-defense requires you to possess a wide range of skills, tactics and techniques. Razing does have its limitations and should be seen as just another tool in your self-defense tool box.

What follows is a list of several situations when razing should not be used.

1. Non Deadly Force situations - As I said earlier, razing can produce serious bodily harm and possible death for your adversary. It is classified as deadly force and must only be used when you are legally justified to use deadly force.

2. Pain compliance situation - Razing should never be used as an intermediate use-of-force response. It's not designed to be a compliance tool to gain control of your opponent.

3. Multiple attacker situations - Successfully defending against multiple attackers requires the freedom to hit and move around your opponents. Unfortunately, razing requires you to commit and anchor to one opponent at a time. Essentially, your mobility is temporarily inhibited.

4. Knife and Edged Weapon Attacks - The number one rule when defending against an edged weapon attack is to always control the weapon first and then neutralize the assailant. Razing a knife wielding adversary with one hand while attempting to control his knife with your other is a foolish action that will almost certainly get you killed.

Exploring Razing Further

    Unfortunately, still photographs don't do justice to the ferocious nature of razing. To truly appreciate the *Widow Maker Program* and witness how fast and devastating razing can be, I encourage you to watch the numerous razing demonstrations featured in my Widow Maker video. It truly is a sight to behold. You can find it on my official website at: ContemporaryFightingArts.com

CHAPTER SIX
Countering Attacks in the Clinch

ENGAGE WITH RAGE

COUNTERING ATTACKS

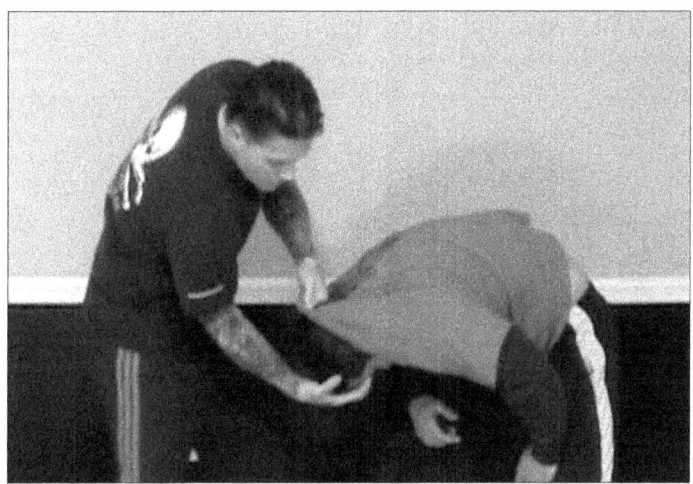

This chapter is going to teach you how to counter an opponent who attempts to negate your clinch fighting skills. Essentially, the techniques that I'm going to teach you are safety valve skills you can apply when your assailant attempts to fight back during your clinch assault.

These advanced techniques include the following:

- *Jersey Pull*
- *Neck Crush*
- *Sharking*
- *Trap and Tuck*
- *Knife Defense*

Once again, it's assumed, at this point, that you're already familiar with the foundational elements of clinching and its related principles and techniques.

Let's begin with the Jersey Pull technique.

JERSEY PULL

Once you have locked up with the adversary in close-quarter combat range, and you have anchored his neck, there's always the chance he might pull away or disengage the clinch. Fortunately, the *Jersey Pull* technique is a very effective way to counter this action.

The Jersey Pull requires you to strategically pull the collar of the assailant's shirt or jacket over his head as he disengages from the clinch.

This technique is ideal because it allows you to maintain control of him while simultaneously impairing his vision. It also permits you to quickly counter attacker with a knee strikes or force him to the ground where you can apply a variety of submission techniques.

Jersey Pull Demonstration

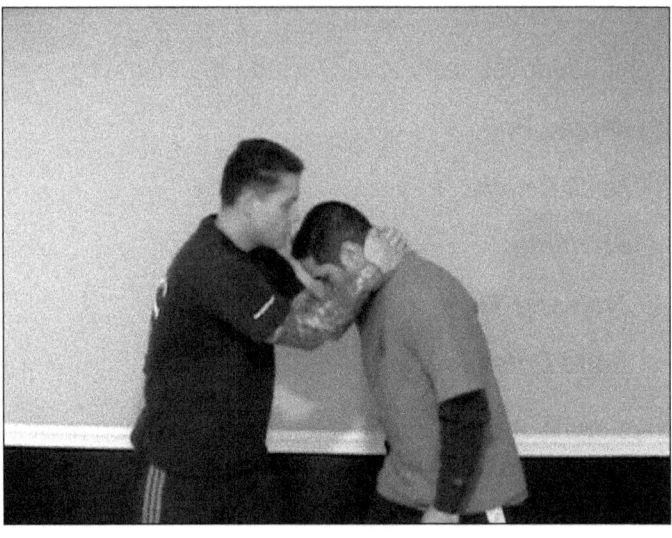

Step 1: Pictured here, Franco anchors his opponent's neck with the neck clamp.

COUNTERING ATTACKS IN THE CLINCH

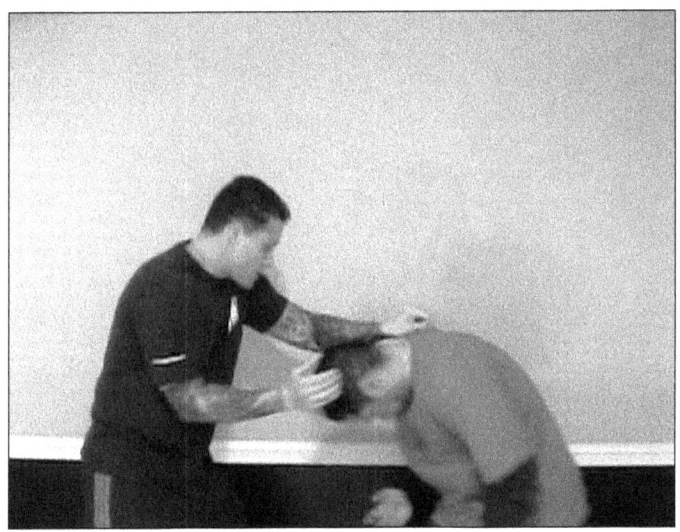

Step 2: The opponent drops his head down to disengages from the clinch.

Step 3: Franco grabs his opponent's collar and pulls it forcefully over his head.

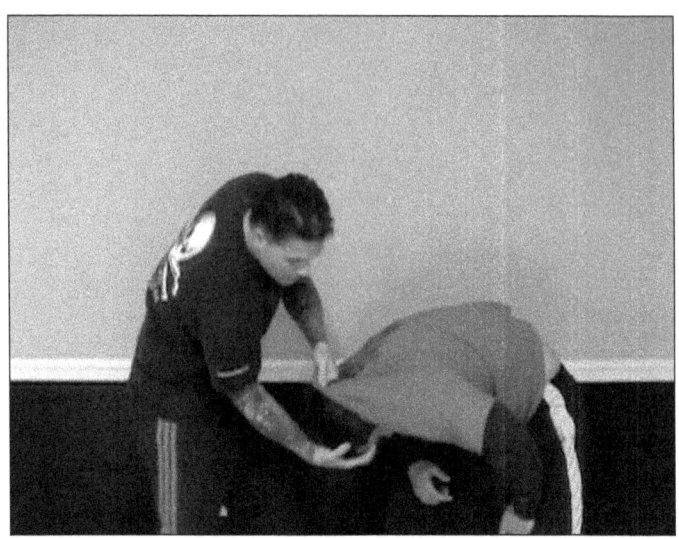

Step 4: He quickly follows up with an eye rake.

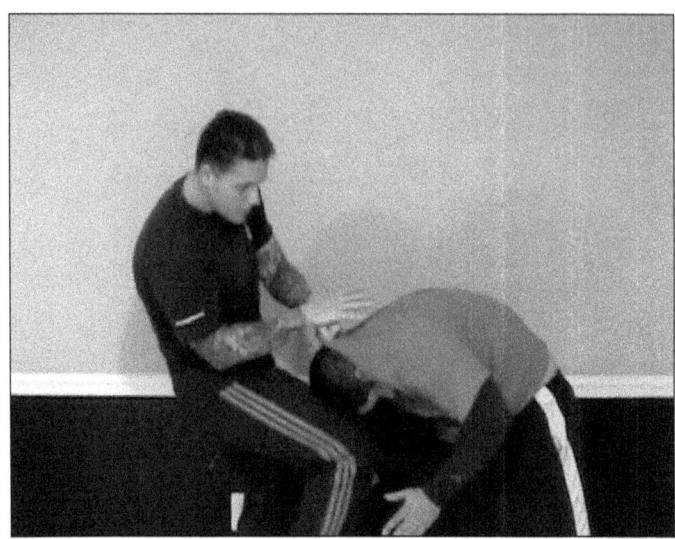

Step 5: Franco finishes his adversary off with a vertical knee strike to the face.

COUNTERING ATTACKS IN THE CLINCH

Jersey Pull to the Ground

The *Jersey Pull* technique can also be used as a quick and effective method of taking your adversary to the ground.

Step 1: The adversary attempts to escape the clinch.

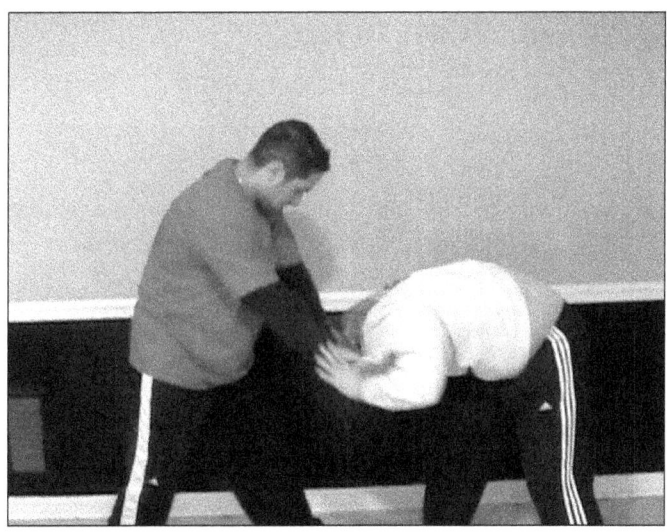

Step 2: The defender (left) applies the Jersey Pull with both hands.

ENGAGE WITH RAGE

Step 3: The defender continues with downward pressure.

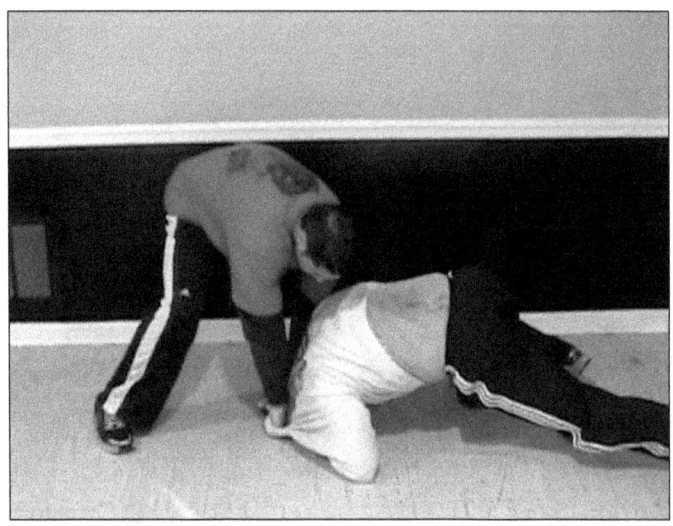

Step 4: The opponent's head crashes to the floor.

COUNTERING ATTACKS IN THE CLINCH

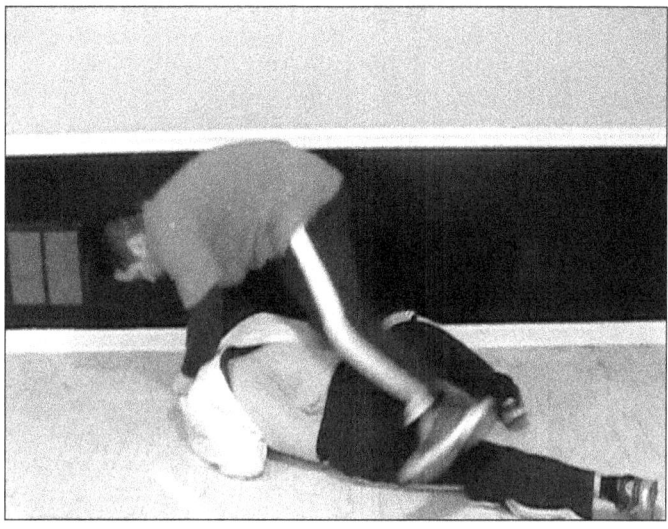

Step 5: The defender quickly repositions himself to the chest to back position.

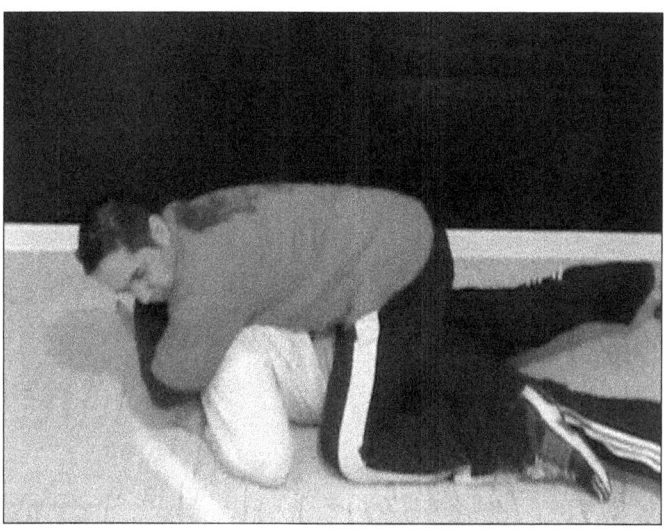

Step 6: The defender mounts his adversary and applies a rear naked choke technique.

Punching Against the Jersey Pull

The following series of photos demonstrates the effectiveness of the jersey pull maneuver against punching techniques. Notice how the opponent doesn't have the balance, leverage, and vision to hit the defender effectively.

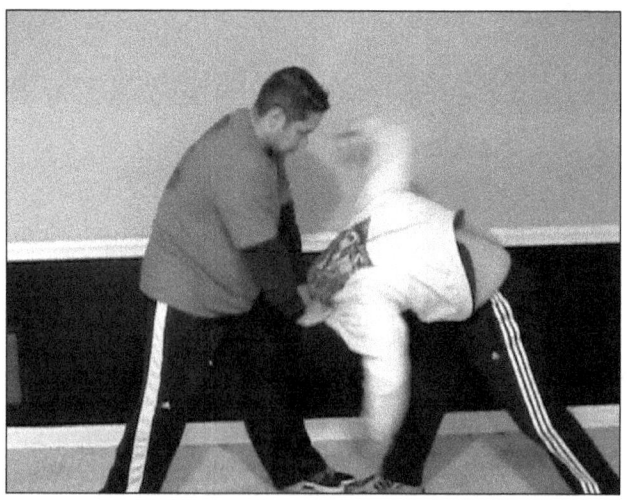

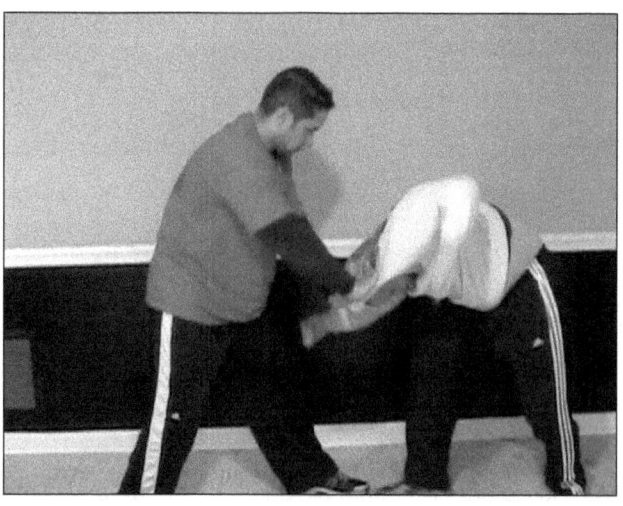

COUNTERING ATTACKS IN THE CLINCH

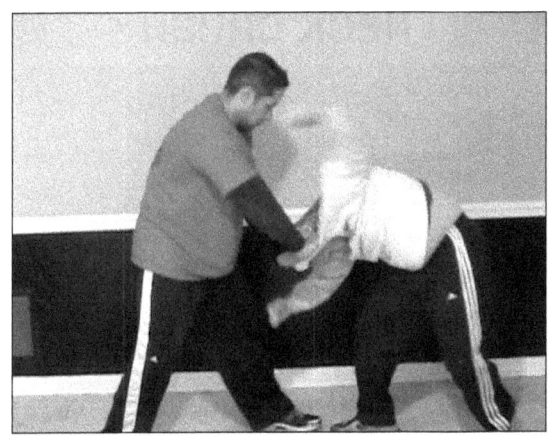

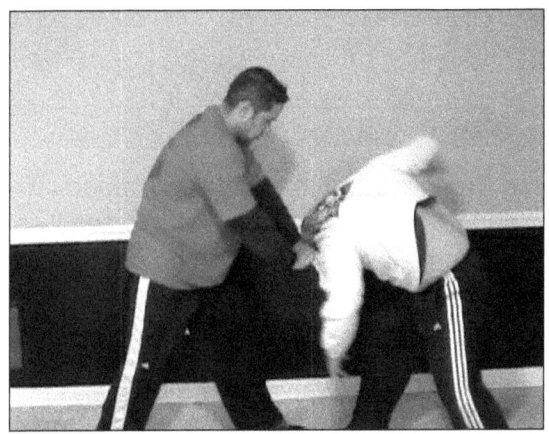

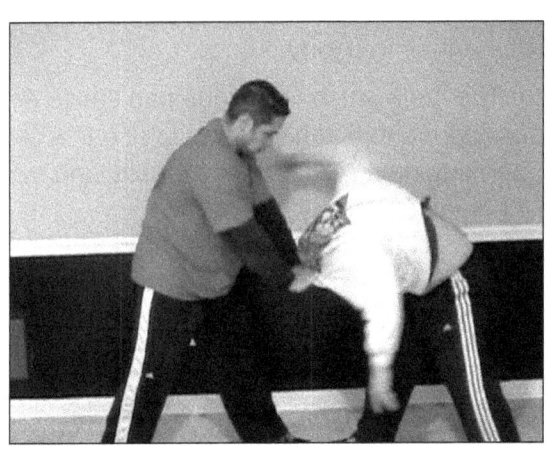

NECK CRUSH

The *Neck Crush* is used to counter an opponent who attempts to negate your clinch assault by forcefully moving his face into your chest. His defensive action drastically limits your hand and wrist movement making it very difficult for you to continue your assault.

Fortunately, the neck crush will counter the opponent's defensive action. Moreover, the neck crush is a very effective pain compliance technique that can quickly drive your adversary to the floor in agony.

Warning! The neck crush technique can cause serious injury to your opponent. If you're going to use this self-defense technique, be certain your actions are legally and morally justified in the eyes of the law!

COUNTERING ATTACKS IN THE CLINCH

Neck Crush Demonstration

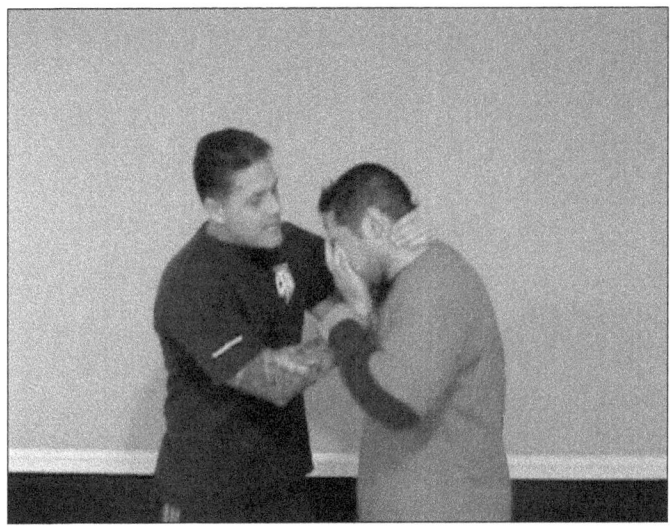

Step 1: Here, the author performs an eye rake from the clinch position.

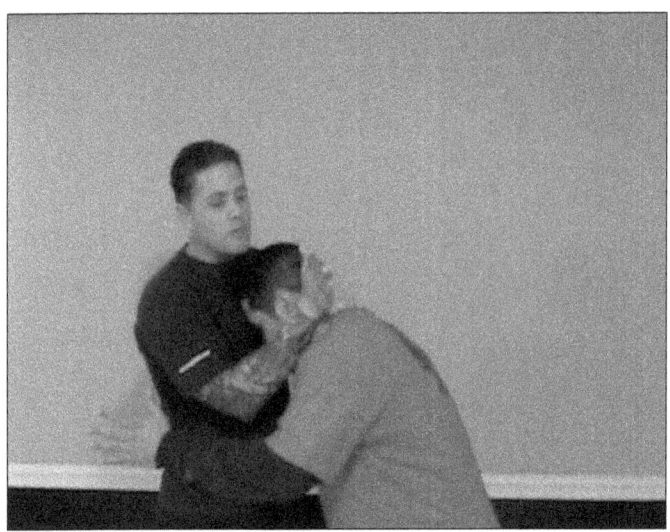

Step 2: The opponent attempts to negate the attack by pulling Franco's hand away and burying his face into his chest.

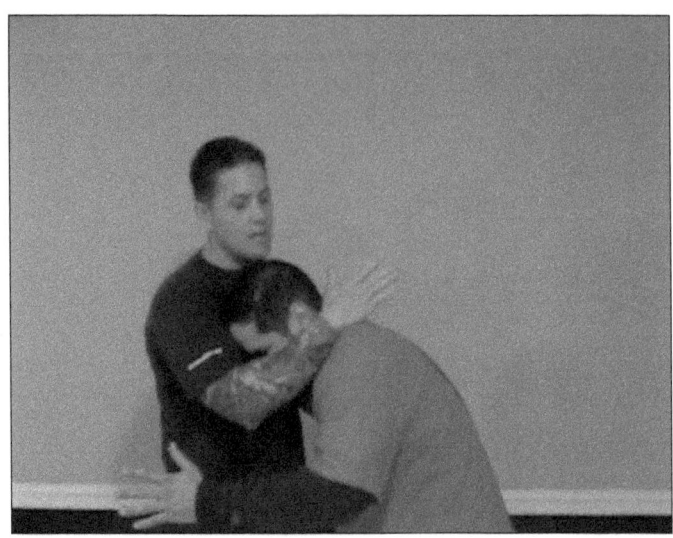

Step 3: Franco forcefully turns his opponent's head sideways.

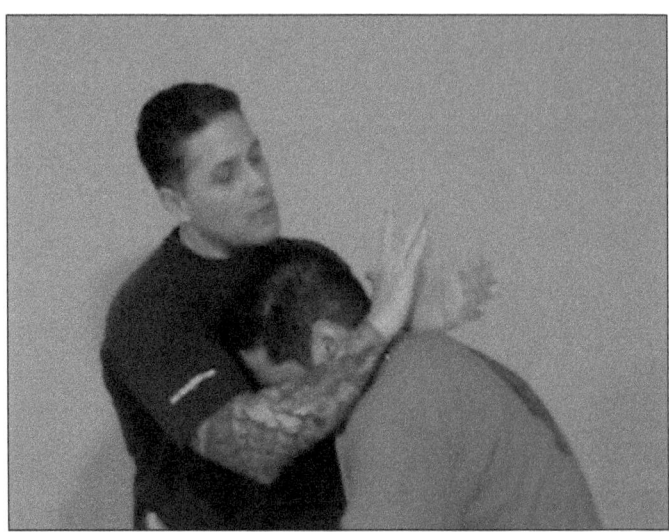

Step 4: Next, he aligns his forearm with the back of the opponent's neck.

COUNTERING ATTACKS IN THE CLINCH

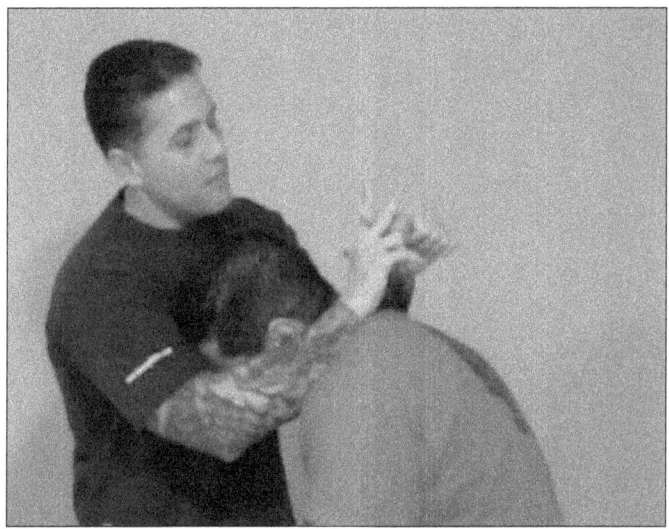

Step 5: Franco inserts his left thumb between the index and middle finger of his right hand (three finger grip).

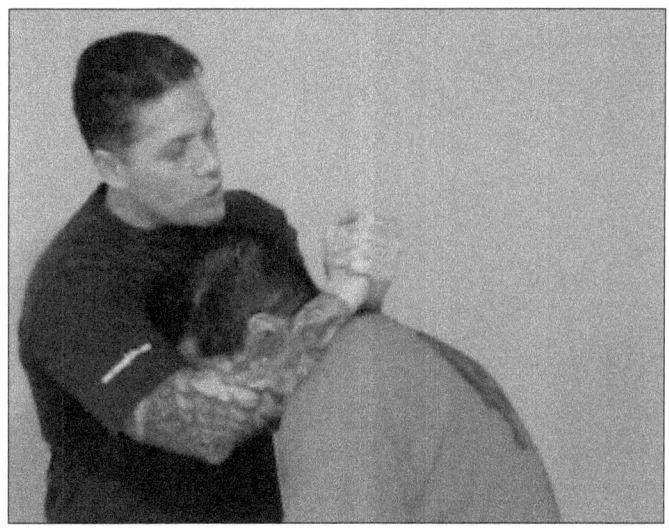

Step 6: He clasps both hands and solidifies the three finger grip.

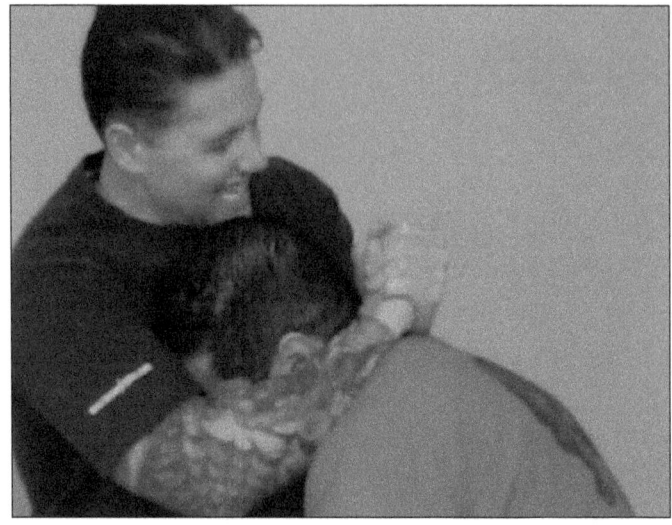

Step 7: Franco forcefully drives the opponent's neck into his chest.

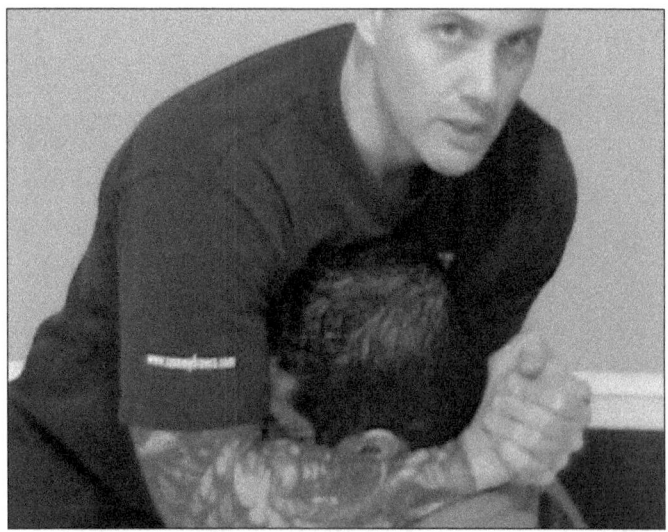

Step 8: Franco takes the opponent down to the ground.

COUNTERING ATTACKS IN THE CLINCH

SHARKING

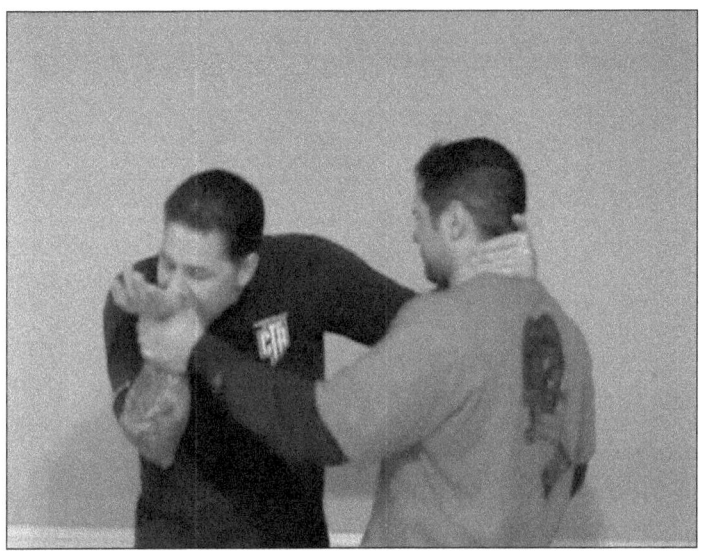

Sharking is designed to counter an adversary who grabs your hand and pulls it away from his face. Sharking is a very effective method of forcing your adversary to release his wrist grab, allowing you to resume your clinch assault.

Sharking is a form of tactical biting that requires you to apply some of the same principles from my *Savage Street Fighting* book.

With the sharking tactic, your objective is to bite the opponent's finger forcefully (usually at the thumb joint) until he releases his hold. Once your hand is free, continue your close-quarter assault.

The following series of photographs will demonstrate the sharking methodology in action.

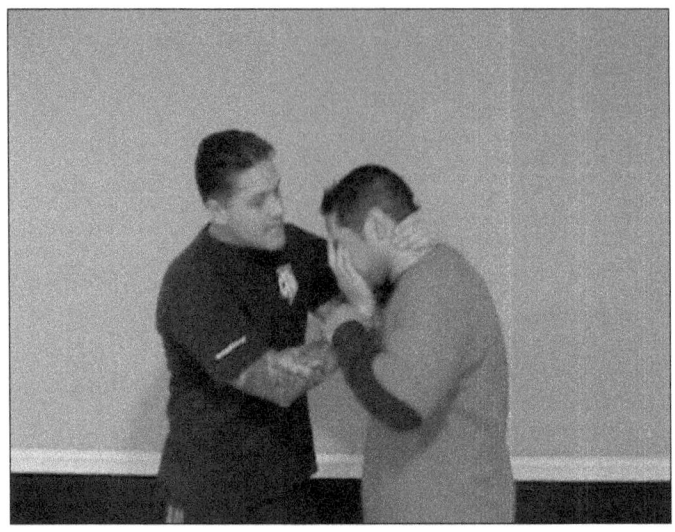

Step 1: Here, the author attacks from the clinch position.

Step 2: The opponent grabs Franco's wrist and pulls it away from his face.

COUNTERING ATTACKS IN THE CLINCH

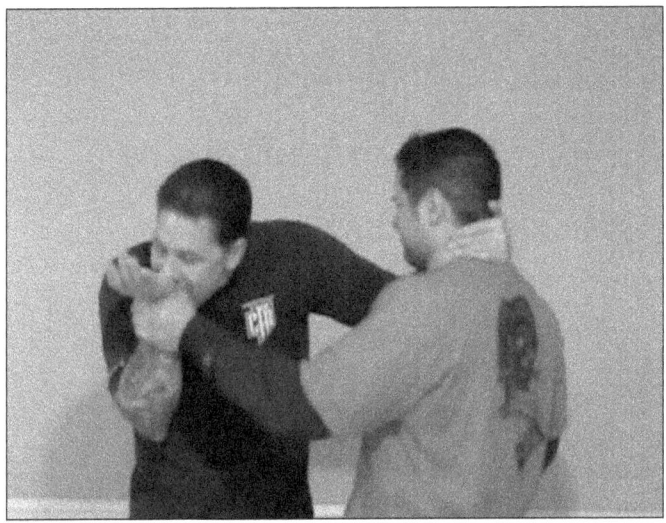

Step 3: While maintaining his anchor, Franco bites forcefully into the opponent's thumb.

Step 4: The opponent immediately releases his hold.

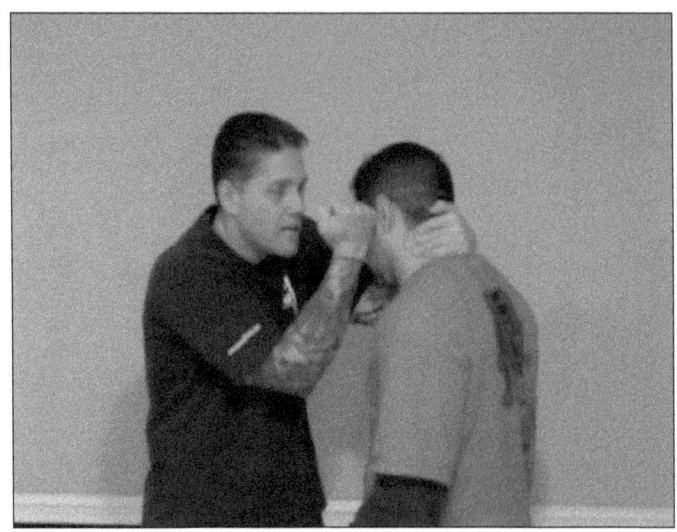

Step 5: Franco resumes his assault with a short arc hammer fist.

COUNTERING ATTACKS IN THE CLINCH

TRAP AND TUCK

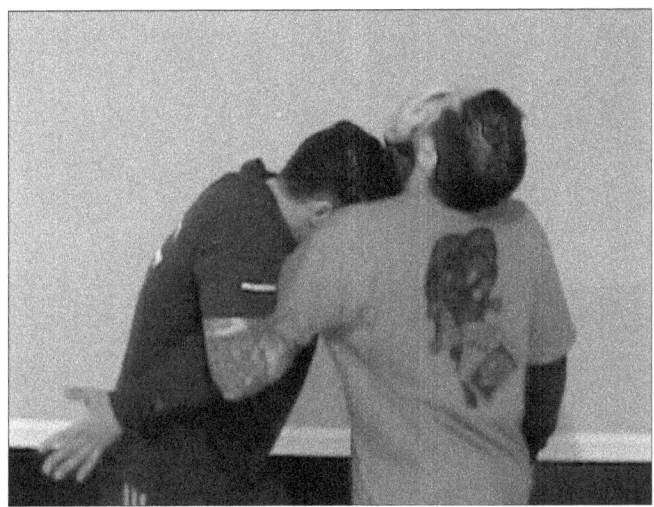

The *Trap and Tuck* technique is used to defend against an opponent who decides to counterattack with his own artless version of Razing.

While an unskilled opponent, who attempts Razing, is more of a nuisance than a serious threat, he still must be dealt with immediately before he becomes a real problem.

The following photo sequence demonstrate the trap and tuck technique during a self-defense encounter.

ENGAGE WITH RAGE

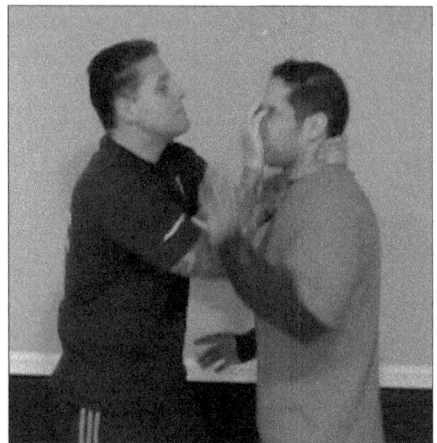

Step 1: Franco begins razing his adversary inside the clinch position.

Step 2: The opponent assumes he can do the same to Franco, and prepares to counter attack.

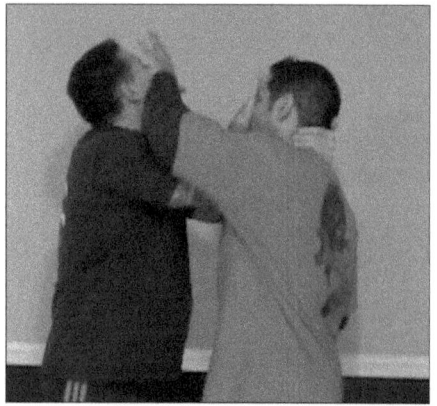

Step 3: In an act of desperation, the opponent attempts to rake Franco's eyes.

COUNTERING ATTACKS IN THE CLINCH

Step 4: Franco immediately employs the trap and tuck technique by securing his opponent's arm using a windmill trapping maneuver.

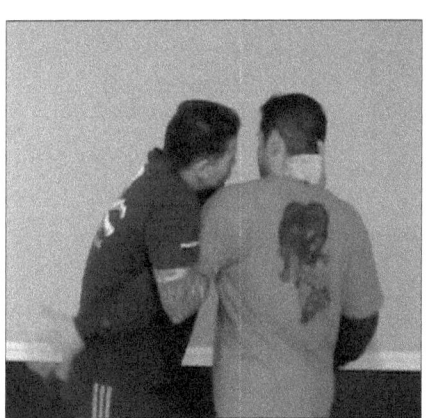

Step 5: He successfully immobilizes his opponent's upper arm.

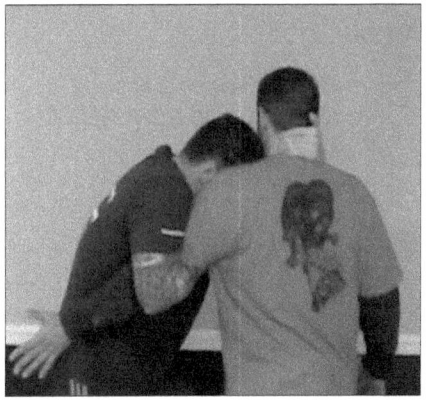

Step 6: Next, Franco tucks his head into his opponent's upper chest region.

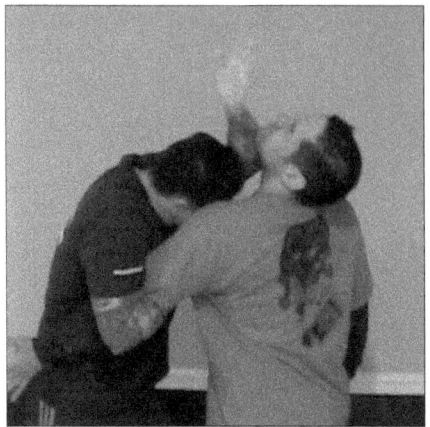

Step 7: Once the Trap and Tuck is successfully implemented, Franco resumes his attack with a vertical elbow to the opponent's chin.

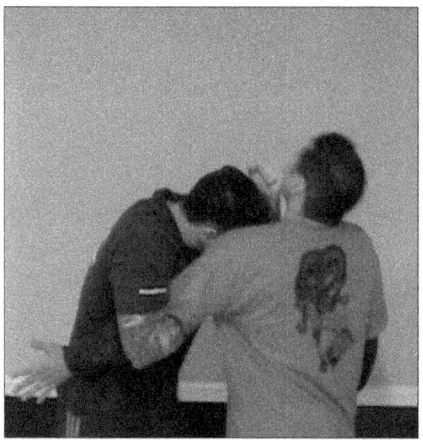

Step 8: Followed by a hammer fist into his opponent's nose.

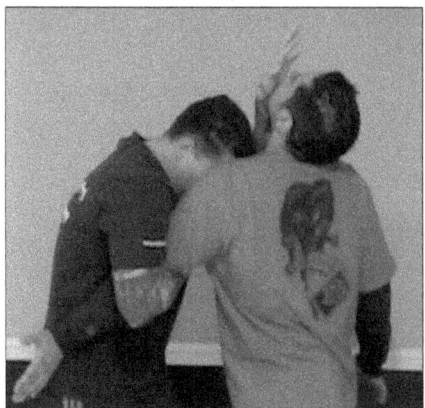

Step 9: Franco's assault is complete with a palm jolt to the chin.

COUNTERING ATTACKS IN THE CLINCH

Trap and Tuck Variation

In the event your adversary attempts to strike you while his arm is trapped, you can apply the following maneuver.

Step 1: Franco blocks the opponent' punch with his free arm.

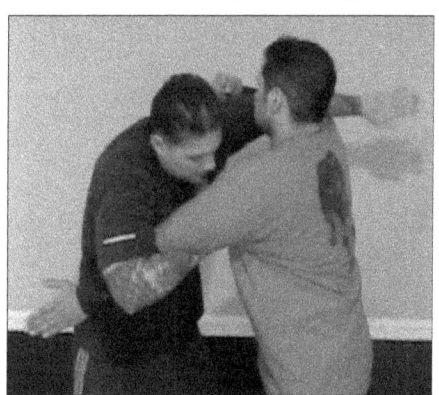

Step 2: Next, he applies another windmill trapping technique.

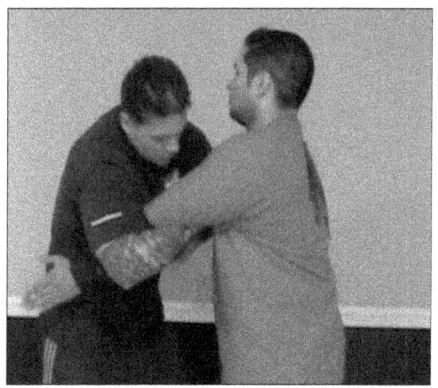

Step 3: Franco now has the option of performing a double arm bar on both of the opponent's elbows, or...

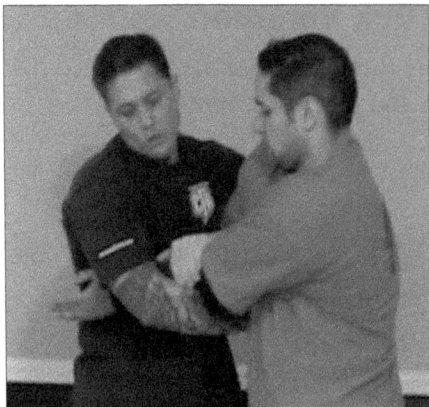

Step 4: He can also thread his left arm across both the opponent's arms and create a figure four lock.

Step 5: With the figure four arm lock in place, Franco has the option to continue his assault on his adversary.

KNIFE DEFENSE IN THE CLINCH

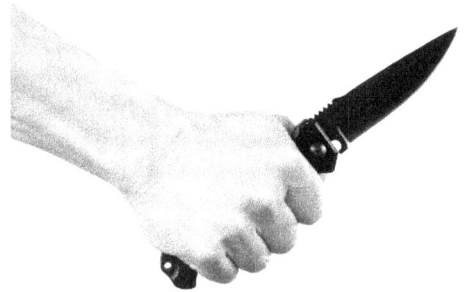

One of the gravest mistakes you can make when clinch fighting is assuming the assailant is unarmed. After all, you never know what will happen during and emergency crisis self-defense situation. There's always the possibility that an edged weapon may rear its ugly little head during the encounter.

Before addressing knife attacks inside the clinch, it's important to go over some of the basic principles of knife defense survival. What follows are some critical concepts:

1. **AVOID IT.** First, it's important to mention that defending against a knife attack is extremely dangerous and should be avoided at all costs. If your situation presents the opportunity to safely escape, <u>do it immediately</u>!

2. **DON'T JUDGE.** When confronted by a knife-wielding assailant, don't assume you can judge his proficiency with the way he or she holds their weapon. Always assume that anyone holding a knife knows how to use it and will do just that. Besides, even if your assailant is unskilled with a knife, he can still kill you.

3. **ASSESS IT.** It's critical to make an accurate threat assessment when confronted by a knife attacker. Use split-second judgment to determine exactly what your adversary wants to accomplish. Some might not want to harm you if

they can avoid it. Others may be dead-set on cutting you from limb to limb. If you have determined that your assailant plans to harm you, you must resort to aggressive disarming tactics.

4. **CREATE DISTANCE.** Try to create as much distance as you can between you and the knife. Distance is critical because it enhances your defensive reaction time and allows you to control your options. Of course, this is going to be difficult if you're locked up in the clinch with the adversary. Nevertheless, running away is a great way to put distance between you and the blade, but you can also use different types of objects in the environment to create barriers between you and your adversary. Cars, trucks, couches, large chairs, tall fences, park benches, and large tables are only a few examples. Remember, though, that these objects are only buying you a little precious time; they don't negate the threat. The bottom line is to stay as far away from the knife as possible. Keep in mind that the only time you want to be close to a knife is for disarming purposes, and then only if the situation is absolutely unavoidable.

5. **DON'T PANIC.** This may seem difficult, but with proper training and crisis rehearsal, it can be done. People naturally freeze up when they're faced with a knife attack. This only makes it easier for your assailant to accomplish his nefarious mission. You must rise to the occasion and summon all of your spirit and courage to ward off the deleterious effects of fear, anxiety, and stress. You must be determined to fight your adversary to the death if necessary.

6. **EXPECT TO GET CUT.** Whether you're unarmed and defending against a knife attack or knife fighting with your adversary, expect to get cut. This frame of mind is critical for the following reasons: (1) it prepares you for the harsh reality of knife combat, (2) it helps prevent you from going

COUNTERING ATTACKS IN THE CLINCH

into mental shock if you do get cut, and (3) it frees you from the mental concern of your well-being.

7. **KNIFE DEFENSE STANCE.** Surviving a knife attack requires mastery of the knife-defense stance. This stance ensures maximal mobility, minimal target exposure, and facilitates immediate counterstrike ability. To assume the knife-defense stance, apply the following steps: (1) angle your body (internal organs) approximately 45 degrees to your assailant; (2) slightly hunch your shoulders forward and let your stomach sink in; (3) keep your head and face back and away from random slashes or stabs; (4) keep your hands, forearms, and elbows close to your body to diminish target opportunities for your assailant; (5) cup your hands with your palms facing you, which will turn soft tissue, veins, and arteries in the arms away from the blade; (6) keep your knees slightly bent and flexible, your feet shoulder-width apart, and your weight equally distributed on each leg; and (7) don't tense up - always stay relaxed and alert.

8. **V-GRIP.** When defending against a knife attack, the only effective method of controlling the assailant's knife hand is to use the V-grip. The V-grip is applied by grabbing the assailant's wrist with both of your hands (make certain that the webs of your hands completely envelope your assailant's wrist). Once you have made contact, squeeze hard and hold on with all your might. When applied correctly, the V-grip allows you to redirect the knife away from your body and counter attack.

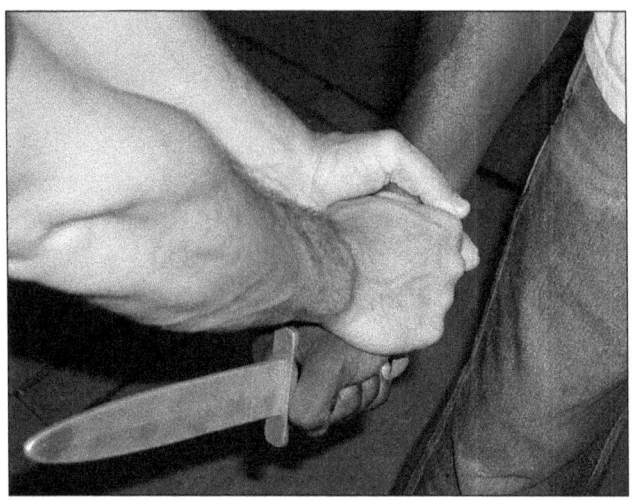

Pictured here, the V-grip.

9. **ATTACK FIRST.** If you're unarmed and faced with a knife-wielding assailant with nowhere to escape, attack him first. This is important for the following reasons: (1) it psyches him out - nothing is more shocking than an unarmed person attacking first, even though the assailant holds all of the cards; (2) it prevents the defensive flow - since you're initiating the attack, it doesn't give your assailant sufficient time to force you into the defensive flow; and (3) it's conclusive - regardless of the outcome, such an act quickly formulates a conclusion to your emergency situation; you have no time to be tormented by despair and fear.

As you might imagine, defending against a knife attack requires mastery of numerous concepts and principles that far exceed the concepts covered in this chapter. However, keep in mind that all of these disarming skills and techniques are set into motion from the knife defense stance.

Having said that, let's take a look at what you can do when faced with a knife attack inside the clinch.

COUNTERING ATTACKS IN THE CLINCH

SWIMMING WITH KNIVES

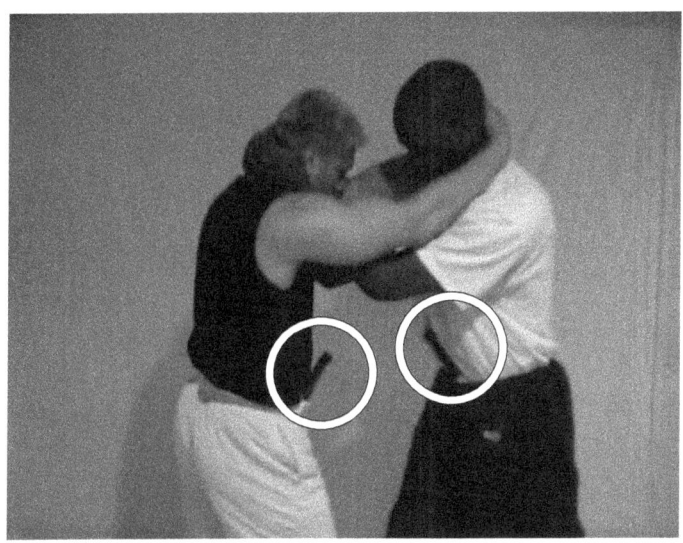

Being able to recognize when your adversary draws a knife from the clinch is critical for street self-defense survival. *Swimming with knives* is one of the best ways to develop edged weapons awareness skills when clinch fighting. This exercise is similar to the basic swimming drill, except this one requires both you and your partner to be armed with a rubber training knife tucked inside your waistband.

Essentially, you would perform the basic swimming drill, along with various clinch strikes… however at any point during the exercise, either one of you can draw your training knife and attack your partner. More advanced practitioners can also steal their partner's knife and stab him with it.

In the event your partner draws his knife first, you must prioritize your defense, abandon the clinch position, and control the knife attack using the V-grip technique discussed earlier. While this drill might seem easy to some people, I can assure you it's not!

Let's take a look at the drill in action.

ENGAGE WITH RAGE

1. The man on the left starts the drill from the outside position.

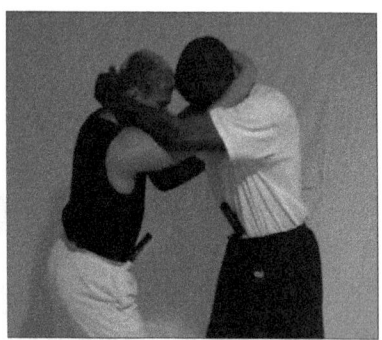

2. He swims his right arm inside the opponent's arm.

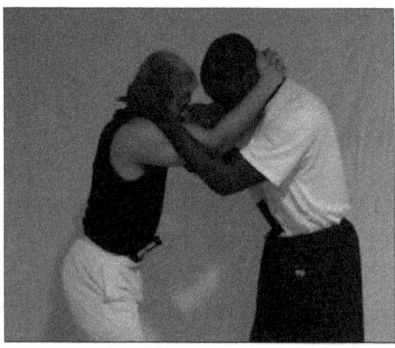

3. Next, he moves his left arm inside his opponent's arm.

4. From the inside position, he simulates a vertical elbow strike.

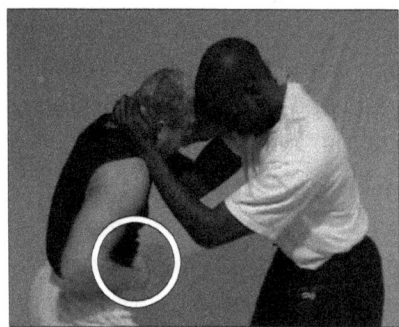

5. He reaches in and draws his knife from his waistband.

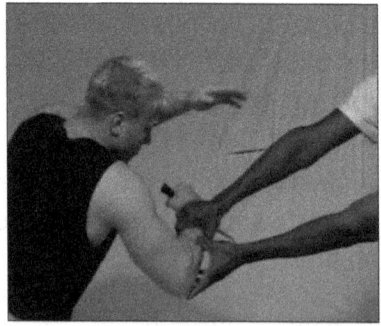

6. His training partner identifies the attack, and V-grips his wrist.

COUNTERING ATTACKS IN THE CLINCH

1. The man on the right starts from the outside position.

2. He swims his left arm inside the opponent's arm.

3. Next, he moves his left arm inside his opponent's arm.

4. From the inside position, he simulates a thumb rake.

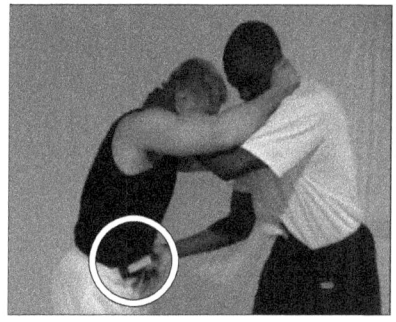

5. He reaches in and snatches his opponent's knife.

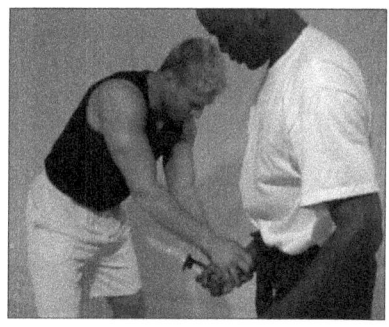

6. His training partner identifies the attack, and V-grips his wrist.

ENGAGE WITH RAGE

1. The man on the left starts the drill from the outside position.

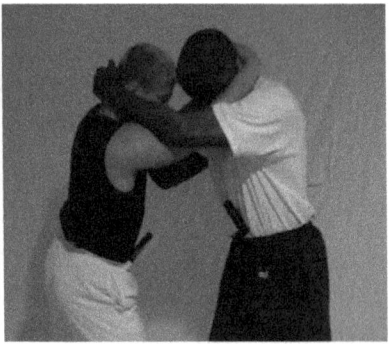

2. He swims his right arm inside the opponent's arm.

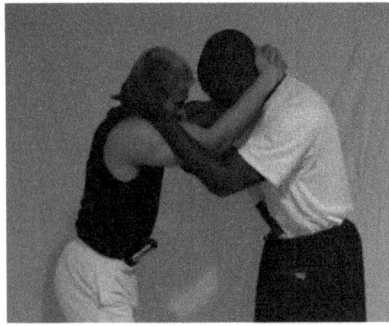

3. Next, he moves his left arm inside his opponent's arm.

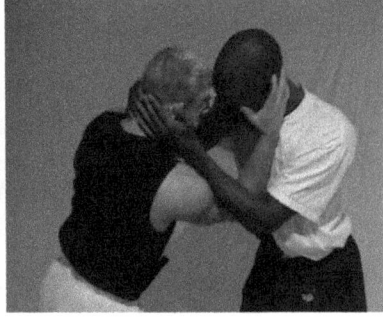

4. From the inside position, he simulates a thumb rake.

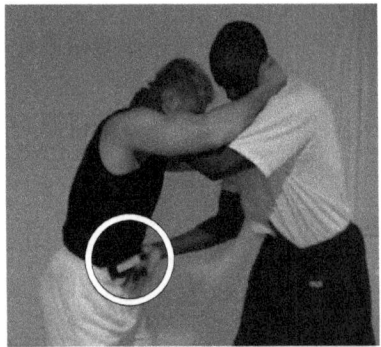

6. His training partner reaches for his knife.

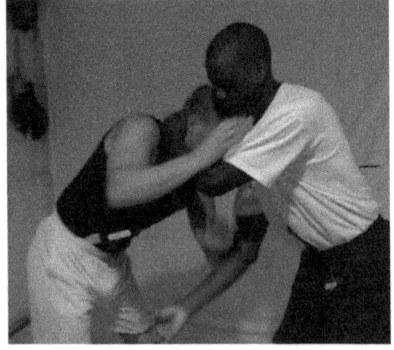

6. He immediately jams his partner's arm with his forearm.

COUNTERING ATTACKS IN THE CLINCH

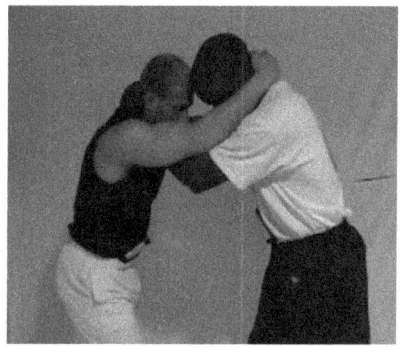

1. The man on the left starts the drill from the outside position.

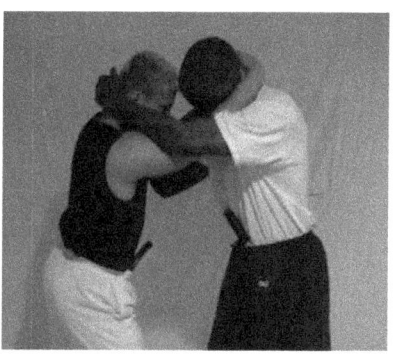

2. He swims his right arm inside the opponent's arm.

3. Next, he moves his left arm inside his opponent's arm.

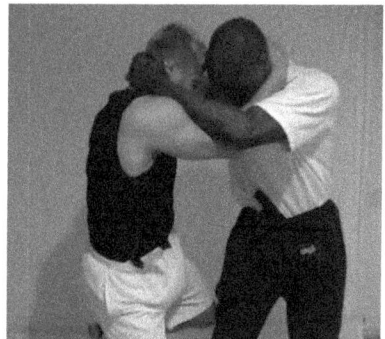

4. From the inside position, he delivers a knee strike.

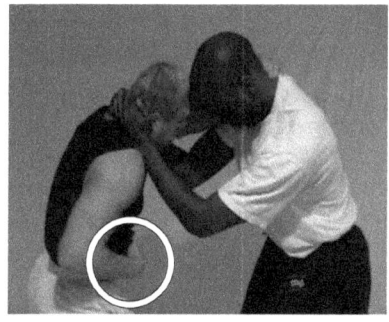

5. He reaches in and draws his knife from his waistband.

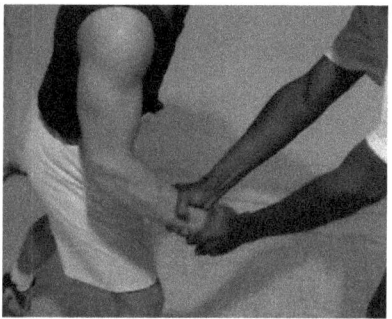

6. His training partner identifies the attack, and V-grips his wrist.

Hard rubber knives are ideal for clinch knife awareness drills.

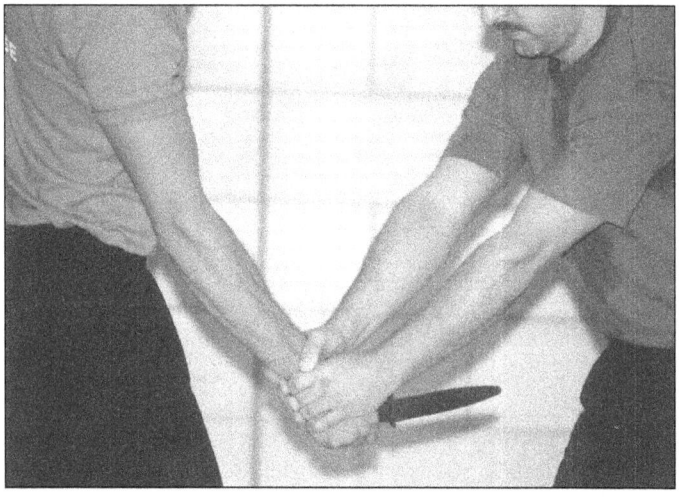

The only effective method of developing knife defense skills is to practice safely with a training partner. When looking to purchase training knives, avoid buying flimsy rubber knives that wiggle when you move them. These knives are cheap and very unrealistic. Always use hard rubber knives or metal training folders.

CAUTION: Be exceptionally careful when slashing at your partner's face with a training knife. To prevent eye injuries, wear some form of eye protection.

CHAPTER SEVEN
Takedown Defenses

ENGAGE WITH RAGE

HOW TO COUNTER THE TAKEDOWN

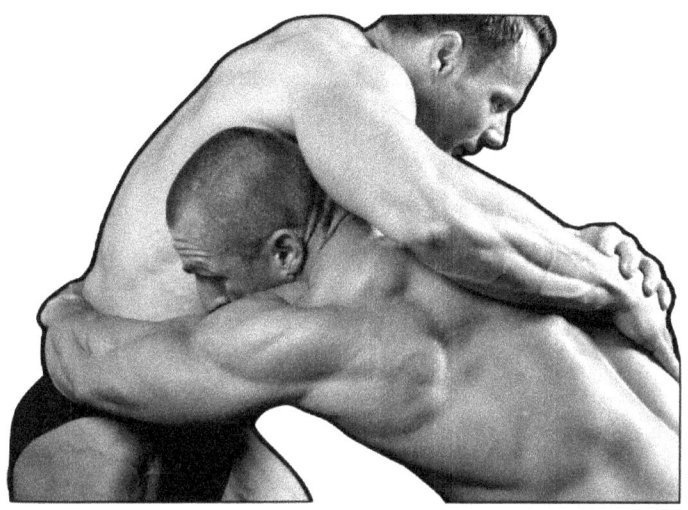

Since this book is devoted entirely to clinch fighting dynamics, it's critically important to cover takedown defenses.

The *takedown* is a staple technique found in just about every fighter's arsenal. For all intents and purposes, a takedown is defined as a technique or maneuver that immediately forces a standing fighter to the ground.

You can be taken down to the ground numerous ways. However, much of it will depend on whom you're fighting. For example, a skilled jiu-jitsu fighter might use a well-executed hip throw while a street punk might attempt a sloppy (but effective) bums rush to take you off your feet.

The type of takedown that your adversary employs can often be influenced by a variety factors such as his fighting style, state of mind, environment, range and proximity.

Regardless of whom you're fighting, your adversary will generally perform a takedown for one of three reasons. They are as follows:

- **Strategic Attack**
- **Desperation Move**
- **Practitioner Error**

Strategic Attack – The takedown is the result of a deliberate and planned method of attack. For example, you and your adversary are fighting in the stand up position; the assailant skillfully defends against your blows, bypasses punching range, locks up with you, sweeps your feet, and takes you to the ground.

Desperation Move – You're beating the hell out of your adversary from the stand up position. He quickly realizes that his stand up fighting skills are grossly deficient and in an act of desperation, grabs hold of you, and takes you to the ground.

Practitioner Error – Takedowns are not always pre-meditated, they can be the residual of a mistake or mishap. For example, your adversary accidentally slips during the course of the stand up fight, grabs hold of you to stabilize his balance, and ends up taking you to the ground with him.

THE STRATEGIC ATTACK

There are six strategic takedowns that are at your opponent's disposal, they are: throwing, tripping, sweeping, locking, striking, and body tackles. Let's take a look at each one.

Throwing Takedowns - The adversary arcs your body through the air before it impacts with the floor (i.e. hip throws, fireman's carry, etc.). Throwing takedowns can be deadly! It's often difficult to recover from a violent throw onto concrete or pavement.

Tripping Takedowns - The adversary strategically plants his leg and pushes you over it.

Sweeping Takedowns - The adversary sweeps your foot, or feet, off the ground through a dynamic motion of his leg.

TAKEDOWN DEFENSES

Locking Takedowns - The adversary locks your joint so he can take you down or throw you to the floor.

Striking Takedowns - The adversary strikes you, causing you to fall to the ground. Striking takedowns are the most indirect form of takedowns.

Body Tackles - The adversary applies pressure or dynamic force (called tackling) to your body or appendage in order to take you down to the ground. Since body tackles are the most common type of takedown, I will focus on them in this chapter.

TAKEDOWN RULE OF THUMB

There's a takedown rule of thumb that most fighters will use in combat. Generally, a fighter will not attempt to "shoot" for a takedown unless you're within his arm's length. In most cases, a fighter is well aware that attempting a takedown beyond his arms reach would be telegraphic and allow you sufficient time to react and counter.

THREE TYPES OF BODY TACKLES

While there are numerous tackles your adversary might employ in a street fight, you should be familiar with the three standard types. They include:

- **Upper body tackle**
- **Mid body tackle**
- **Lower body tackle**

Upper Body Tackle - this is also known as the "bum's rush". There's nothing sexy or scientific about this particular tackle. It is simply a matter of the adversary rushing and grabbing you with a bear hug (your arms can be either trapped or free).

Essentially, it's the momentum of the opponent's bodyweight that knocks you off balance and forces you to the ground. Upper body tackles can come from both the front, side, or rear (such as an ambush attack).

Pictured here, the upper body tackle.

TAKEDOWN DEFENSES

Mid Body Tackle - also called a "waist tackle". The opponent rushes forward, ducks under your arms and tackles you at the waist. Keep in mind that many lay people are skilled at this type of tackle because of recreational football training. Once again, the momentum of the opponent's bodyweight will knock you off balance and take you to the ground.

Lower Body Tackle - Lower body tackles can come in the form of either single or double leg tackles. For example, to

perform the single leg tackle, the fighter lowers his base, shoots forward to your lead leg and grabs behind your knee. He then drives his shoulder into your hip and takes you to the ground. Both the single and double leg takedown requires the greatest amount of skill to successfully execute in a self-defense situation.

BALANCE IS EVERYTHING!

If you haven't figured it out by now, in order for your adversary to take you down to the ground, he must first disrupt or break your balance. Generally, there are four ways he can accomplish this task. They are the following:

Redirection of Force - Occurs when your adversary exploits your energy or dynamic pressure and disrupts your balance.

Strength Manipulation - Your adversary uses his raw power and sheer strength to disrupt your balance.

Striking Impact - Your assailant hits you, causing a reaction dynamic that throws you off balance.

Feinting or Faking - Your assailant feints, draws a defensive reaction from you that throws you off balance.

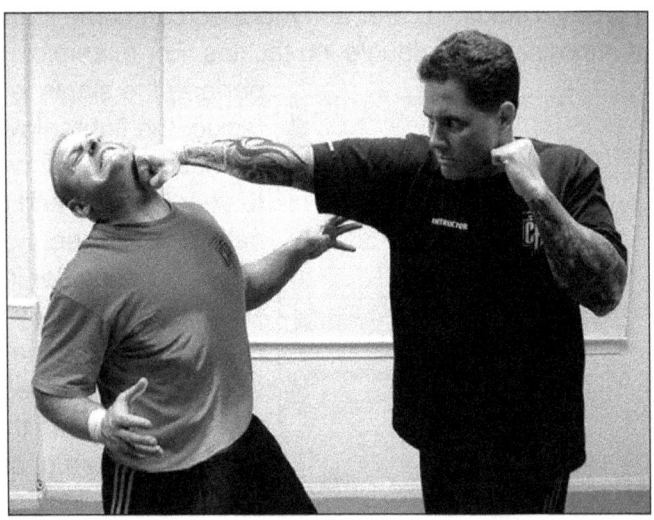

Striking Impact is one of the four ways you can lose your balance causing you to end up on the ground.

TAKEDOWN DEFENSES

THE STABILITY DRILL

The *stability drill* is excellent for learning how to maintain your balance once the adversary has grabbed hold of you. This exercise will also get you accustomed to the critical importance of proper weight shifting by developing your sense of tactile sensitivity.

To begin the drill, square off with your training partner at the grappling range. Then grab hold of each other (you can grab the wrists, elbows, arms, shoulders, the nape of the neck, and waist).

Next, have your partner (the designated attacker) initiate the drill by pulling and pushing you in various directions in an effort to throw you off balance.

Grab hold of him and try to stabilize your balance while he is pulling and pushing. Try to quickly adapt to the intense and unpredictable nature of his energy.

This drill can get very intense and can last up to five minutes in duration. Advanced self defense practitioners can also perform this exercise while blindfolded.

In this photo, two students perform the stability drill.

ENGAGE WITH RAGE

YOU NEED A STANCE

Before you can apply the actual defensive moves against a takedown, you'll first need a solid stance. While just about any stance will work with these anti-grappling techniques, one of the best to use is my de-escalation stance.

The De-escalation stance is used during the pre-contact phase of unarmed combat. The proper de-escalation stance (for kicking & punching ranges) can be acquired first blading your body at approximately 45-degrees from the adversary. Then keep both of your feet approximately shoulder-width apart and have your knees slightly bent with your weight evenly distributed.

Both of your hands are open, relaxed, and up to protect the upper targets. Keep your torso, pelvis, head, and back erect and stay relaxed and alert - while remaining at ease and in total control of your emotions and body.

Remember to avoid any muscular tension—don't tighten up your shoulders, neck, arms, or thighs (tension restricts breathing and quick evasive movement, and it will quickly sap your vital energy).

5 TAKEDOWN DEFENSES

Now that you have a rudimentary understanding of the three body tackles and you have a good stance, it's time to take the next step and learn some takedown defenses. In my CFA system, we have five different types of takedown defenses. They include the following:

- **Range Manipulation**
- **Height Change to Level of Entry**
- **Stiff-Arm Jam**
- **Webbing**
- **Sprawling**

Range Manipulation

As the name implies, range manipulation is the strategic manipulation of fighting ranges. If you recall, I mentioned earlier in this chapter that a knowledgeable fighter will most likely attempt a takedown only if you are within his arms reach (approximately punching range).

Therefore, one of the best ways to delay being taken to the ground is to stay outside of the fighter's "shooting range" with quick and responsive footwork. This will keep the range open and prevent the grappler from setting up an effective takedown. Incidentally, the term "shoot" or "shooting" means an explosive forward movement (generally low level) while grabbing the legs with the sole objective of taking a person to the ground.

Footwork Basics

The safest footwork for combat involves quick, economical steps performed on the balls of your feet, while you remain relaxed and balanced. When moving on the balls of your feet, always try to keep your legs a shoulder-width apart and your weight evenly distributed. Moving on the balls of your feet does not mean haphazardly dancing around your assailant. This type of "show boating" will get you into serious trouble. Remember to always move with a strategic purpose in mind. Basic footwork is structured around four general directions:

Forward (advance) - from your stance, first move your front foot forward (approximately twelve inches) and then move your rear foot an equal distance.

Backward (retreat) - from your stance, first move your rear foot backward (approximately twelve inches) and then move your front foot an equal distance.

Right (sidestep right) - from your stance, first move your right foot to the right (approximately twelve inches) and then move your left foot an equal distance.

Left (sidestep left) - from your stance, first move your left foot to the left (approximately twelve inches) and then move your right foot an equal distance.

Basic footwork skills should also be practiced from two different states: Static and Ballistic. Static footwork movements are executed from a static or stationary position; while ballistic footwork movements are executed while you are moving. Do not forget to practice footwork maneuvers with different types of footwear. For example, combat boots, hiking boots, running shoes, dress shoes, cross trainer shoes, sandals, cowboy boots and loafers). In addition, practice footwork skills when you're barefoot.

Range Manipulation Drill

The range manipulation drill is a simple yet effective exercise that will improve your range awareness and sharpen your reflexes.

To perform the drill, have both you and your training partner take turns setting up the takedown while the other quickly opens up the range before he can move in. Perform this drill for 10-15 minutes.

Height Change to Level of Entry

A solid and effective takedown will also require your adversary to lower his base to get his hips under you. This means he will need to bend at his knees and back to lower his *level of entry*. When your adversary gets within his "shooting range" and lowers his level of entry, it's critical for you to immediately match his height change. This action will dramatically reduce the effectiveness of his takedown.

One of the best weight training exercises for improving your height change reflexes is the squat. The squat is a fantastic exercise that builds mass and strength in the thighs. To perform the exercise do the following:

1. With you feet approximately shoulder width apart and in front of your hips, rest a barbell across the back of your shoulders while holding it in place with both hands.

2. While keeping your head up, back straight and your feet flush against the floor, slowly bend your knees and lower your body until your thighs are parallel to the ground.

3. Push yourself back to the starting position. Perform five sets of 8-10 repetitions preferably two times per week.

One of the best weight training exercises for improving your height change reflexes is the squat.

When confronted with a fighter who is about perform a takedown, be certain to adjust to his level of entry. Notice how the fighter on the left has lowered his height (height change) prior to shooting in for the takedown.

TAKEDOWN DEFENSES

Stiff-Arm Jam Technique

The stiff-arm jam is a very effective method of negating the destructive force of both the upper and mid body tackles.

To perform the technique, simultaneously lower your base (height change to level of entry) and extend both of your arms forward. Both of your palms should make contact with the assailant's upper chest and shoulder. Be certain to pull your fingers back to avoid accidental sprains or breaks. Your objective is to instantaneously negate or jam the overwhelming force of the takedown.

If your adversary attempts the upper body tackle, the palms of your hands should make contact on both sides of his chest region. If the grappler attempts a mid body tackle, lower your base and have your palms jam him at his shoulders.

Step1: The fighter on the left attempts a takedown.

Step 2: As the adversary moves in to tackle, the practitioner on the right immediately lowers his height to match the opponent's level of entry. He negates the fighter's forward momentum with a stiff-arm jam to the upper chest area.

TAKEDOWN DEFENSES

Step 3: Once the stiff-arm jam negates the fighter's momentum, the defender moves in and engages the clinch position.

Step 4: The defender delivers a head butt strike to his assailant's nose.

ENGAGE WITH RAGE

STIFF-ARM JAM FLOW DRILL

To make the stiff arm jam more instinctual under combat conditions, you can integrate it with a flow drill.

Step 1: The practitioners begin the drill with the man on the left initiating a tight overhead strike. The man on the right blocks it.

Step 2: After blocking the strike, he uses his right arm to redirect his partner's arm.

TAKEDOWN DEFENSES

Step 3: As the man on the right redirects his partners arm, he slaps it downward with his left hand.

Step 4: The man on the right then strikes his partner with a tight overhead strike.

Step 5: Next, the man on the left blocks his partner's hit.

Step 6: He redirects his partner's arm with his right hand.

TAKEDOWN DEFENSES

Step 7: Instead of slapping his partner's hand, the man on the left moves in with an upper body tackle. The man on the right immediately counters with a stiff arm jam.

Step 8: He follows up with a horizontal elbow strike.

Webbing Against The Takedown

The Webbing technique was first introduced in 2003 through our Widow Maker Program. This offensive based technique is utterly devastating and should only be used when deadly force is legally and morally justified.

At first glance, webbing looks like a reinforced palm heel strike. However, there's much more to it. It requires specific hand and arm articulation, proper body mechanics, and correct timing. However, once mastered, Webbing will feel natural and will become an instinctual body weapon that can be deployed under the stress of a deadly criminal attack.

Webbing is both an offensive and defensive technique that can disable any opponent of any size. Interestingly enough, I termed this technique *Webbing* because your hands resemble a large web that wraps around the enemy's face.

What follows is a detailed breakdown of the proper body mechanics for effective Webbing. Keep in mind that you must not forget to change your height to match your assailant's level of entry. Also, remember that proper Webbing body mechanics are executed in one explosive movement that should take less than one second to execute.

TAKEDOWN DEFENSES

1. From a left lead (your left leg is forward) stance. Simultaneously overlap your left hand on top of your right hand. Your right thumb should be aligned under the 5th metacarpal of your left hand (see picture). Your right palm is the striking surface while your left reinforces the structural integrity of the strike.  The left hand is also particularly important because it significantly reduces the likelihood of a wrist or hand injury and it magnifies the power of the blow.

2. Once the hands are properly joined, forcefully extend both arms into the enemy's chin. Your elbows should also be slightly bent when impacting with the target. Do not lock your elbows. Unlike conventional punches, your body does not torque when launching the Webbing strike. Destructive power comes from synergistically utilizing your major muscle groups (i.e., back, chest, shoulders and triceps) accompanied with forward momentum.

3. The ideal trajectory of the Webbing blow should be approximately 45-degrees to the enemy's chin. Remember, you're trying to transmit shock waves to the cerebellum and cerebral hemispheres of the assailant's brain. Once again, take into account that the angle of impact may change depending on the assailant's height change and level of entry. Make certain that both of your palms are approximately perpendicular to the floor.

4. You can launch the Webbing strike while remaining stationary, however forward momentum will increase the power exponentially. Forward momentum can be generated in one of two ways: the half step or the full step.

5. Finally, once the two hands make contact with the target, allow both hands to split apart and engage the clinch using the neck clamp technique.

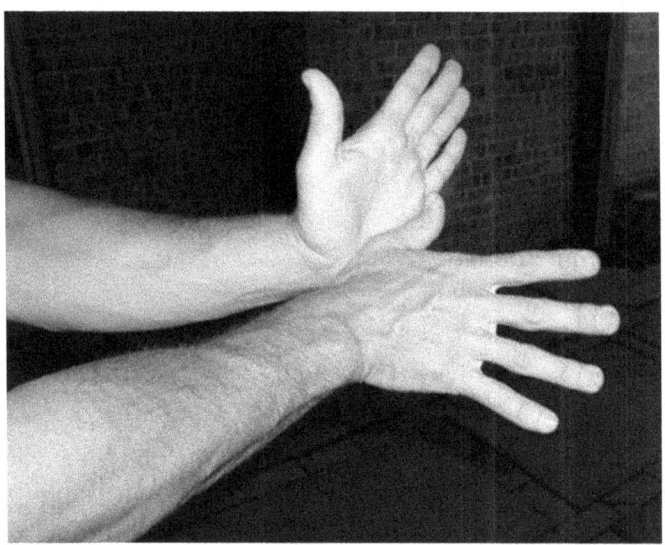

Step 1: Your right thumb should be aligned under the 5th metacarpal of your left hand.

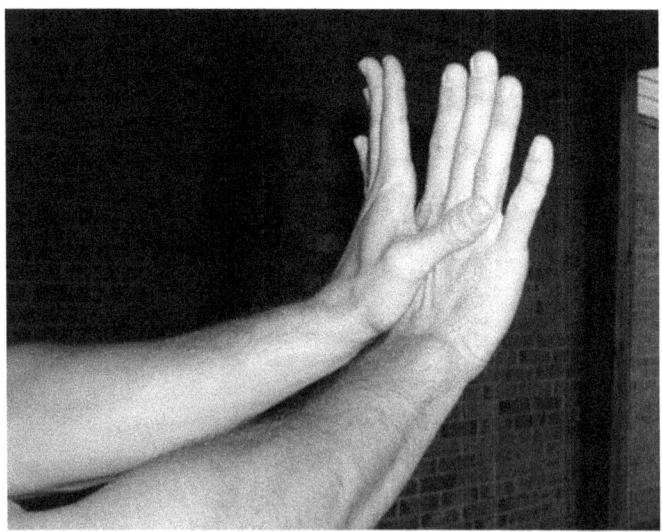

Step 2: Your left hand reinforces the structural integrity of the strike.

TAKEDOWN DEFENSES

Webbing Demonstration

Step 1: Begin from a de-escalation stance.

Step 2: Simultaneously overlap your left hand on top of your right hand. Your right thumb should be lined under the 5th metacarpal of your left hand.

ENGAGE WITH RAGE

Step 3: Once your hands are properly joined, forcefully extend both of your arms forward.

Step 4: Drop your head slightly downward as you step forward.

Step 5: Your elbows are slightly bent when impacting with the target.

TAKEDOWN DEFENSES

Webbing (front view)

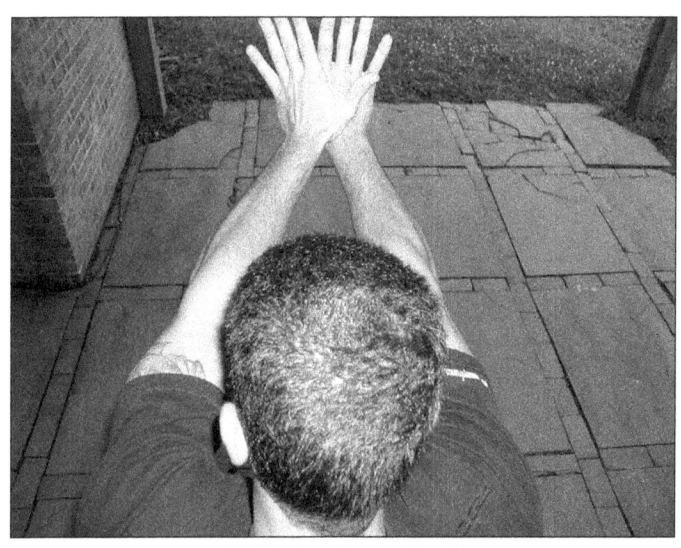

Webbing (rear view)

Sprawling Against The Tackle

Sprawling is a defensive technique used to negate a takedown attempt. More specifically, it's used to counter both mid and lower body tackles and it's particularly effective against the single and double leg takedown.

Essentially, sprawling negates the penetration of the assailant's takedown by spreading your legs back and driving your hip into his head and shoulder. When properly executed, sprawling will place you on top of your opponent's back.

When sprawling, make certain to maintain steady pressure on the opponent's back, and square your hips as you arch them away from the adversary.

Step 1: In this photo, the fighter (right) attempts a mid body tackle. The self-defense practitioner (left) immediately sprawls his legs back and drops his hips into the grappler's head and shoulders.

TAKEDOWN DEFENSES

Step 2: The defender (left) maintains steady pressure, which drives his opponent straight to the ground.

Step 3: The defender (top) quickly pivots and rotates his body around the grappler's back.

ENGAGE WITH RAGE

Step 4: Finally, the defender executes a modified neck choke to incapacitate his adversary.

CHAPTER EIGHT
Clinch Conditioning

ENGAGE WITH RAGE

CLINCH CONDITIONING

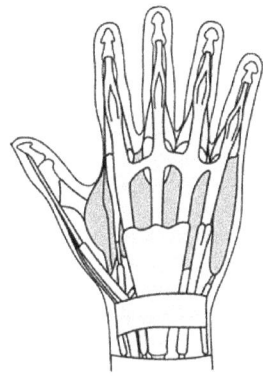 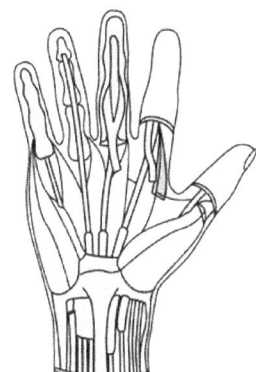

It's no surprise that strong fingers, wrists and forearms will significantly enhance your clinch fighting skills. Powerful hands and forearms will also amplify the power of your rakes, gouges, and tearing techniques. Strong forearms will enhance techniques such as neck cranks, rear naked chokes, and anchoring. There are several effective hand and forearm exercises you can perform to strengthen these muscles.

What follows are several ways to condition and strengthen your hands, wrists and forearms.

Power Putty

One excellent hand exerciser that strengthens all the muscles in your fingers and hands is Power Putty. Essentially, Power Putty is a flexible silicone rubber that can be squeezed, stretched, and crushed. Begin using the putty for ten minute sessions and progressively build up to thirty minutes.

This tough resistant putty will strengthen the muscles of your forearm, wrists, hands and fingers. Remember to work both hands equally.

Hand Grippers

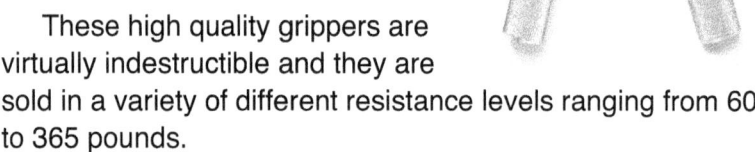

Another effective way to strengthen your hands, wrists and forearms is to work out with heavy duty hand grippers. While there are a wide selection of them on the market, I personally prefer using the Captains of Crush brand.

These high quality grippers are virtually indestructible and they are sold in a variety of different resistance levels ranging from 60 to 365 pounds.

IronMind EGG

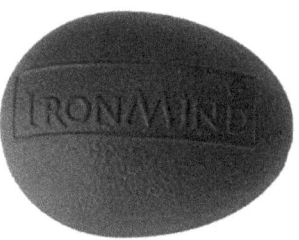

This is another great tool for strengthening and conditioning your hands. Made of a 21st century polymer, the IronMind EGG will add a new dimension to your grip training.

Tennis Ball

If you are low on cash and just starting out with your training, you can begin by squeezing a tennis ball a couple times per week. One hundred repetitions per hand would be a great start.

Weight Training

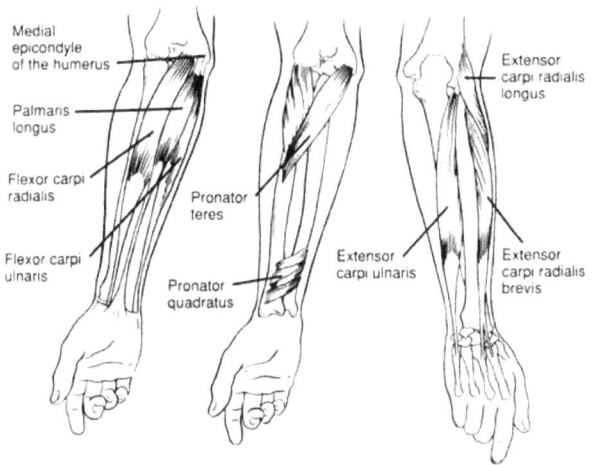

Finally, you can also condition your wrists and forearms by performing various forearm exercises with free weights. Exercises like hammer curls, reverse curls, wrist curls, and reverse wrist curls are great for developing powerful forearms. When training your forearms, be certain to work both your extensor and flexor muscles. Let's look at some of the exercises.

Barbell Wrist Curls

This exercise strengthens the flexor muscles. Perform 5 sets of 8-10 repetitions. To perform the exercise, follow these steps:

1. Sit at the end of a bench, grab a barbell with an underhand grip and place both of your hands close together.

2. In a smooth and controlled fashion, slowly bend your wrists and lower the barbell toward the floor.

3. Contract your forearms and curl the weight back to the starting position.

Reverse Wrist Curls

This exercise develops and strengthens the extensor muscle of the forearm. Perform 6 sets of 6-8 repetitions. To perform the exercise, follow these steps:

1. Sit at the end of a bench, hold a barbell with an overhand grip (your hands should be approximately 11 inches apart) and place your forearms on top of your thighs.

2. Slowly lower the barbell as far as your wrists will allow.

3. Flex your wrists upward back to the starting position.

Behind-the-Back Wrist Curls

This exercise strengthens both the flexor muscles of the forearms. Perform 5 sets of 6-8 repetitions To perform the exercise, follow these steps:

1. Hold a barbell behind your back at arm's length (your hands should be approximately shoulder-width apart).

2. Uncurl your finger and let the barbell slowly roll down your palms.

3. Close your hands and roll the barbell back into your hands.

Hammer Curls

This exercise strengthens both the Brachialis and Brachioradialis muscles. Perform 5 sets of 8-10 repetitions. To perform the exercise, follow these steps:

1. Stand with both feet approximately shoulder width apart, with both dumbbells at your sides.

2. Keeping your elbows close to your body and your palms facing inward, slowly curl both dumbbells upward towards your shoulders.

3. Slowly return to the starting position.

Reverse Barbell Curls

Reverse curls can be a great alternative to hammer curls. This exercise strengthens both the Brachialis and Brachioradialis muscles. Perform 5 sets of 8-10 repetitions. To perform the exercise, follow these steps:

1. Stand with both feet approximately shoulder width apart. Hold a barbell with your palms facing down (pronated grip).

2. Keeping your upper arms stationary, curl the weights up until the bar is at shoulder level.

3. Slowly return to the starting position.

General Combat Conditioning

Finally, if you want to maximize the efficiency and effectiveness of your clinch fighting skills, you must be physically fit. Fitness and conditioning comprises the following three broad components: cardiorespiratory conditioning, muscular/skeletal conditioning, and proper body composition.

The cardiorespiratory system includes the heart, lungs, and circulatory system, which undergo tremendous stress in a high-risk situation. So you're going to have to run, jog, bike, swim, or skip rope to develop sound cardiorespiratory conditioning. Each aerobic workout should last a minimum of 30 minutes and be performed at least four times per week.

The second component of conditioning is muscular/skeletal conditioning. To strengthen your bones and muscles to withstand the rigors of combat, your training must include progressive resistance (weight training). You will also need a stretching program designed to loosen up every muscle group. As I said earlier, stretching on a regular basis will also increase the muscles' range of motion, improve circulation, reduce the possibility of injury and relieve daily stress.

    The final component of conditioning is proper body composition: simply, the ratio of fat to lean body tissue. Your diet and training regimen will affect your level or percentage of body fat significantly. A sensible and consistent exercise program accompanied by a healthy and balanced diet will facilitate proper body composition.

GLOSSARY

Many of the terms in this book may be strange to the first time reader. This is because most of the lexicon in this text are unique only to Contemporary Fighting Arts. What follows are some important terms often used in my CFA system.

A

Accuracy - The precise or exact projection of force. Accuracy is also defined as the ability to execute a combative movement with precision and exactness.

Action - A series of moving parts that permit a firearm to be loaded, unloaded and fired.

Adaptability - The ability to physically and psychologically adjust to new or different conditions or circumstances of combat.

Aerobic Exercise - "With air." Exercise that elevates the heart rate to a training level for a prolonged period of time, usually 30 minutes.

Affective Domain - This includes the attitudes, philosophies, ethics, values, discretionary use-of-force, and the spirit (killer instinct) required to use your combative tool or technique appropriately.

Affective Preparedness - Being emotionally and spiritually prepared for the demands and strains of combat.

Aggression - Hostile and injurious behavior directed toward a person.

Aggressive Hand Positioning - Placement of hands so as to imply aggressive or hostile intentions.

Aggressive Stance - (See Fighting Stance.)

Aggressor - One who commits an act of aggression.

Agility - An attribute of combat. One's ability to move his or her body quickly and gracefully.

Amalgamation - A scientific process of uniting or merging.

Ambidextrous - The ability to perform with equal facility on both the right and left sides of the body.

Ambush - To lie in wait and attack by surprise.

Ambush Zones - Strategic locations (in everyday environments) from which assailants launch surprise attacks.

American Stick Strangle - A stick strangle used with a hammer grip.

Analysis and Integration - One of the five elements of CFA's mental component. This is the painstaking process of breaking down various elements, concepts, sciences, and disciplines into their atomic parts, and then methodically and strategically analyzing, experimenting, and drastically modifying the information so that it fulfills three combative requirements: efficiency, effectiveness and safety. Only then is it finally integrated into the CFA system.

Anatomical Handles - Various body parts (i.e., appendages, joints, and in some cases, organs) that can be grabbed, held, pulled or otherwise manipulated during a ground fight.

Anatomical Power Generators - Three points on the human body that help torque your body to generate impact power. Anatomical Power Generators include: (1) Feet; (2) Hips; (3) Shoulders.

Anatomical Striking Targets - The various anatomical body targets that can be struck and which are especially vulnerable to potential harm. They include: the eyes, temple, nose, chin, back of neck, front of neck, solar plexus, ribs, groin, thighs, knees, shins, and instep.

Arm Lock - A joint lock applied to the arm.

Assailant - A person who threatens or attacks another.

GLOSSARY

Assault - The willful attempt or threat to inflict injury upon the person of another.

Assault and Battery - The unlawful touching of another person without justification.

Assert - One of the five possible tactical responses to a threatening situation. To stand up for your rights (see Comply, Escape, De-Escalate, and Fight Back).

Assessment - The process of rapidly gathering, analyzing, and accurately evaluating information in terms of threat and danger. You can assess people, places, actions, and objects.

Attachment - The touching of the arms or legs prior to executing a trapping technique.

Attack - Offensive action designed to physically control, injure, or kill another person.

Attack By Draw - One of the five conventional methods of attack. A method of attack whereby the fighter offers his assailant an intentional opening designed to lure an attack.

Attributes of Combat - The physical, mental, and spiritual qualities that enhance combat skills and tactics.

Attribute Uniformity - Various combative attributes (i.e., speed, power, accuracy, balance, etc.) which are executed the same way every time.

Autoloader - A handgun that operates by mechanical spring pressure and recoil force that ejects the spent cartridge case and automatically feeds a fresh round from the magazine. (Also known as a Semiautomatic).

Awareness - Perception or knowledge of people, places, actions, and objects. (In CFA there are three categories of tactical awareness: Criminal Awareness, Situational Awareness, and Self-Awareness.)

Axiom - A truth that is self-evident.

B

Back Position - One of the ground fighting positions. The back position is assumed when your chest is on top of your assailant's back.

Back fist - A punch made with the back of the knuckles.

Back strap - The rear, vertical portion of the pistol frame.

Balance - One's ability to maintain equilibrium while stationary or moving.

Barrier - Any large object that can be used to obstruct an attacker's path or angle of attack.

Blading the Body - Strategically positioning your body at a 45-degree angle.

Block - A defensive tool designed to intercept the assailant's attack by placing a non-vital target between the assailant's strike and your vital body target.

Bludgeon - Any club like weapon used for offensive and defensive purposes (e.g., baseball bat, club, pipe, crowbar, heavy tree branch, etc.) Bludgeons are usually heavier and thicker than sticks.

Body Composition - The ratio of fat to lean body tissue.

Body Language - Nonverbal communication through posture, gestures, and facial expressions.

Body Mechanics - Technically precise body movement during the execution of a body weapon, defensive technique, or other fighting maneuver.

Body Weapon - One of the various body parts that can be used to strike or otherwise injure or kill a criminal assailant. (Also known as Tool).

Bore - The inside of the barrel of a firearm.

Boxing - (See Western Boxing).

Break fall - A method of safely falling to the ground.

Burn Out - A negative emotional state acquired by physically over training. Some symptoms of burn-out include: physical illness, boredom, anxiety, disinterest in training, and general sluggish behavior.

Bushido - The ancient and honorable code of the samurai or warrior.

C

Cadence - Coordinating tempo and rhythm to establish a timing pattern of movement.

Caliber - The diameter of a projectile.

Cardiorespiratory Conditioning - A component of physical fitness that deals with the heart, lungs, and circulatory system.

Carriage - The way you carry yourself.

Cartridge - A cylindrical case containing components of a round of ammunition: case, primer, powder charge, and bullet.

Center-Fire - A type of firearm cartridge that has its primer located in the center of the case bottom.

Centerline - An imaginary vertical line that divides your body in half and which contains many of your vital anatomical targets.

Center Mass - The center portion of the torso.

Chamber - 1) The part of a firearm in which a cartridge is contained at the instant of firing. 2) The raising of the knee to execute a kick.

Choice Words - (See Selective Semantics.)

Choke - A close quarter (grappling range) technique that requires one to apply pressure to either the trachea of carotid arteries.

Circular Movement - Movements that follow the direction of a curve.

Close Quarter Combat - One of the three ranges of knife and bludgeon combat. At this distance, you can strike, slash, or stab your assailant with a variety of close-quarter techniques.

Close to Contact Shooting - Discharging a firearm with the muzzle approximately one inch distance from the target.

Cognitive Development - One of the five elements of CFA's mental component. The process of developing and enhancing your fighting skills through specific mental exercises and techniques. (see Analysis and Integration, Killer Instinct, Philosophy and Strategic/Tactical Development.)

Cognitive Domain - This encompasses the specific concepts, principles and knowledge required to use your combative tools or techniques effectively.

Cognitive Exercises - Various mental exercises used to enhance fighting skills and tactics.

Combat Arts - The various arts of war. (See Martial Arts.) Combative Attributes - (See Attributes.)

Combative Fitness - A state characterized by cardiorespiratory and muscular/ skeletal conditioning, as well as proper body composition.

Combative Mentality - A combative state of mind necessary for fighting. Also known as the Killer Instinct. (see Killer Instinct.)

Combat Ranges - The various ranges of armed and unarmed combat.

Combative Power - The ability of capacity to perform or act effectively in combat.

Combative Truth - A combative element that conforms to fact or actuality and which is proven to be true.

Combative Utility - The quality of condition of being combatively useful. Combination(s) - (See Compound Attack.)

Come-Along - A series of holds or joint locks that force your adversary to move in any direction you desire.

GLOSSARY

Coming to a Base - The process of getting up to your hands and knees from the prone position.

Common Peroneal Nerve - A pressure point area located approximately four to six inches above the knee on the midline of the outside of the thigh.

Completion Phase - One of the three stages of a stick or bludgeon strike. The completion phase is the completion point of a swing.

Comply - One of the five tactical responses to a threatening situation. To obey an assailant's demands. (see Assert, De-Escalate, Escape, and Fight Back.)

Composure - A combative attribute. Composure is a quiet and focused mind set that enables you to acquire your combative agenda.

Compound Attack - One of the five conventional methods of attack. Two or more body weapons launched in strategic succession whereby the fighter overwhelms his assailant with a flurry of full speed, full force blows. (see Indirect Attack, Immobilization Attack, Attack By Draw, and Single Attack.)

Concealment - Not being visible to your adversary.

Conditioning Training - A CFA training methodology requiring the practitioner to deliver a variety of offensive and defensive combinations for a four minute period (see Proficiency Training and Street Training.)

Confrontation Evasion - Strategically manipulating the distance or environment to avoid a possible confrontation.

Congruency - The state of harmoniously orchestrating the verbal and non verbal de-escalation principles.

Contact Evasion - Physically moving or manipulating your body targets to avoid being struck (i.e., slipping your head to the side or side stepping from a charging assailant).

Contact Shooting - Discharging a firearm with the muzzle touching the target.

Contemporary Fighting Arts® (CFA) - A modern martial art and self-defense system made up of three parts: physical, mental, and spiritual.

Conventional Ground Fighting Tools - Specific ground fighting techniques designed to control, restrain and temporarily incapacitate your adversary. Some conventional ground fighting tactics include: submission holds, locks, certain choking techniques, and specific striking techniques.

Cool-down - A series of light exercises and movements that immediately follow a workout. The purpose of the cool-down is to hasten the removal of metabolic wastes and gradually return the heart to its resting rate.

Coordination - A physical attribute characterized by the ability to perform a technique or movement with efficiency, balance, and accuracy.

Counterattack - Offensive action made to counter an assailant's initial attack.

Courage - A combative attribute. The state of mind and spirit that enables a fighter to face danger and vicissitudes with confidence, resolution, and bravery.

Courageousness - (See Courage).

Cover - Any object that protects you from gunfire.

Criminal Awareness - One of the three categories of CFA awareness. It involves a general understanding and knowledge of the nature and dynamics of a criminal's motivations, mentalities, methods, and capabilities to perpetrate violent crime. (see Situational Awareness and Self-Awareness.)

Criminal Justice - The study of criminal law and the procedures associated with its enforcement.

Criminology - The scientific study of crime and criminals.

Criss Cross - An entry maneuver which allows you to travel across a threshold quickly while employing a correct ready

GLOSSARY

weapon position.

Cross Stepping - The process of crossing one foot in front or behind the other when moving.

Crushing Tactics - Nuclear grappling range techniques designed to crush the assailant's anatomical targets.

Cutting Accuracy - The ability to cut your assailant with precision and exactness.

Cutting Makeshift Weapon - One of the four types of CFA makeshift weapons. Any object or implement that can be used to effectively stab or slash an assailant. (see also Distracting Makeshift Weapon, Shielding Makeshift Weapon, and Striking Makeshift Weapon.)

Cylinder - The part of a revolver that holds cartridges in individual chambers.

D

Deadly Force - Weapons or techniques that may result in imminent, unconsciousness, permanent disfigurement, or death.

Deadly Weapon - An instrument designed to inflict serious bodily injury or death (e.g., firearms, impact tools, edged weapons).

Deception - A combative attribute. A stratagem whereby you delude your assailant.

Decisiveness - A combative attribute. The ability to follow a tactical course of action that is unwavering and focused.

De-escalation - One of the five possible tactical responses to a threatening situation. The science and art of diffusing a hostile individual without resorting to physical force. (see Assert, Comply, Escape and Fight Back).

De-escalation Stance - One of the many strategic stances used in the CFA system. A strategic and non aggressive stance used when diffusing a hostile individual.

Defense - The ability to strategically thwart an assailant's attack (armed or unarmed).

Defensive Flow - A progression of continuous defensive responses. Defensive Mentality - A defensive mind-set.

Defensive Range Manipulation (DRM) - The strategic manipulation of ranges (armed or unarmed) for defensive purposes.

Defensive Reaction Time - The elapsed time between an assailant's physical attack and your defensive response to that attack (see Offensive Reaction Time).

Demeanor - One of the essential factors to consider when assessing a threatening individual. A person's outward behavior.

Dependency - The dangerous phenomenon of solely relying on a particular person, agency, instrument, device, tool, animal, or weapon for self-defense and personal protection.

Destructions - A technique that strikes the assailant's attacking limb. Diet - A life-style of healthy eating.

Distance Gap - The spatial gap between the different ranges of armed and unarmed combat.

Distancing - The ability to quickly understand spatial relationships and how they relate to combat.

Distracting Makeshift Weapon - One of the four types of CFA makeshift weapons. An object that can be thrown into an assailant's face, body, or legs to distract him temporarily (see Cutting Makeshift Weapon, Striking Makeshift Weapon, and Shielding Makeshift Weapon.)

Distraction Tactics - Various verbal and physical tactics designed to distract your adversary.

Dojo - The Japanese term for "training hall."

Dominant Eye - The eye which is primarily used for aiming a firearm. The dominant eye is the one which is stronger and does more work.

Double-Action - A type of pistol action in which squeezing the trigger will both cock and release the hammer.

Drake Shooting - Shooting into places of likely cover.

Dry Firing - The process of shooting an unloaded firearm.

Duck - A defensive technique that permits you to evade your assailant's strike. Ducking is performed by dropping your body down and forward to avoid the assailant's blow.

E

Ectomorph - A body type classified by a high degree of slenderness, angularity, and fragility (see Endomorph and Mesomorph).

Effectiveness - One of the three criteria for a CFA body weapon, technique, tactic or maneuver. It means the ability to produce a desired effect (see Efficiency and Safety).

Efficiency - One of the three criteria for a CFA body weapon, technique, tactic or maneuver. It means the ability to reach an objective quickly and economically (see Effectiveness and Safety).

Ejector - The part of a pistol which ejects empty cartridge cases.

Embracing the Range - A ground fighting tactic whereby you pull or embrace your assailant.

Emotional Control - One of the nonverbal principles of strategic de-escalation. The ability to remain calm when faced with a hostile or threatening person.

Emotionless - A combative attribute. Being temporarily devoid of human feeling.

Endomorph - A body type classified by a high degree of roundness, softness, and body fat (see Ectomorph and Mesomorph).

Entry Method - A method that permits you to safely enter a

combat range. Entry Technique - A technique that permits you to safely enter a combat range.

Entry Tool - A tool that permits you to safely enter a combat range.

Escape - Also known as tactical retreat. One of the five possible tactical responses to a threatening situation. To flee rapidly from the threat or danger. (See Comply, De-Escalate, Assert and Fight Back).

Escape Routes - Various avenues or exits that permit you to escape from a threatening individual or situation.

Evasion - A defensive maneuver that allows you to strategically maneuver your body away from the assailant's strike.

Evasive Sidestepping - Evasive footwork where the practitioner moves to either the right or left side.

Evasiveness - A combative attribute. The ability of avoid threat or danger. Evolution - A gradual process of change.

Excessive Force - An amount of force that exceeds the need for a particular event and is unjustified in the eyes of the law.

Experimentation - The painstaking process of testing a combative hypothesis or theory.

Explosiveness - A combative attribute that is characterized by a sudden outburst of violent energy.

F

Fake - Body movements that disguise your attack. This includes movements of the eyes, head, shoulders, knees, feet and in some cases the voice.

Fatal Funnel - A danger area that is created by openings such as doorways, windows, hallways, stairwells, etc.

Feed - (See Attachment.)

GLOSSARY

Fear - A strong and unpleasant emotion caused by the anticipation or awareness of threat or danger. There are three stages of fear in order of intensity: Fright, Panic, and Terror. (see Fright, Panic, Terror).

Feeler - A tool that tests the assailant's reaction time and overall abilities.

Feint - A tool that draws an offensive reaction from the assailant, thereby opening him up for a real strike. Feints are different from fakes because they are performed through the movement of an actual limb.

Femoral Nerve - A pressure point area located approximately six inches above the knee on the inside of the thigh.

Fight Back - One of the five possible tactical responses to a threatening situation. To use various physical and psychological tactics to either incapacitate or terminate a criminal assailant. (See Comply, Escape, Assert and De-Escalate.)

Fighting Stance - One of the different types of stances used in CFA's system. A strategic posture you can assume when face-to-face with an unarmed assailant (s). (See De-escalation Stance, Knife Defense Stance, Knife Fighting Stance, Firearms Stance, Natural Stance, Stick Fighting Stance).

Fight-or-Flight Syndrome - A response of the sympathetic nervous system to a fearful and threatening situation, during which it prepares your body to either fight or flee from the perceived danger.

Finesse - A combative attribute. The ability to skillfully execute a movement or a series of movements with grace and refinement.

Firearm Follow Through - Continuing to employ the shooting fundamentals throughout the delivery of your shot.

First Strike Principle (FSP) - A CFA principle which states

that when physical danger is imminent and you have no other tactical option but to fight back, you should strike first, strike fast, and strike with authority.

Flexibility - The muscles' ability to move through maximum natural ranges (see Muscular/Skeletal Conditioning).

Follow - A defensive technique used in the mid to long range of knife combat.

Forms - Traditional martial arts training methodology whereby the practitioner performs a series of prearranged movements that are based upon a response to imaginary opponents (see Kata).

Formlessness - A principle that rejects the essence of structure or system.

Footwork - Quick, economical steps performed on the balls of the feet while you are relaxed, alert, and balanced. Footwork is structured around four general movements: forward, backward, right, and left.

Fractal Cognizance - Being knowledgeable and aware of the fractal ranges and tools of combat.

Fright - The first stage of fear; quick and sudden fear (see Panic and Terror).

G

Gi - A traditional martial art uniform constructed of heavy cotton canvas material. The gi is commonly worn by practitioners of karate, judo, aikido, and jujitsu.

Grappling Range - One of the three ranges of unarmed combat. Grappling range is the closest distance of unarmed combat from which you can employ a wide variety of close-quarter tools and techniques. The grappling range of unarmed combat is also divided into two different planes: vertical (standing) and horizontal (ground fighting). (see Kicking Range and Punching Range)

Grappling Range Tools - The various body tools and techniques that are employed in the grappling range of unarmed combat, including head butts; biting, tearing, clawing, crushing, and gouging tactics; foot stomps, horizontal, vertical, and diagonal elbow strikes, vertical and diagonal knee strikes, chokes, strangles, joint locks, and holds. (see and Kicking Range Tools).

Grapevine - A stabilizing technique used during a ground fight. The grapevine can be applied when you have either one (single leg grapevine) or both (double leg grapevine) of your feet hooked around the assailant's legs.

Ground Fighting - Fighting that takes place on the ground. (Also known as horizontal grappling plane).

Guard - 1) A fighter's hand positioning. 2) One of the positions used in ground fighting. The guard is a scissors hold applied with the legs.

H

Hammer - The moving part of a gun causes the firing pin to strike the cartridge primer.

Hammer Grip - A hand grip used to hold an edged weapon, bludgeon and some makeshift weapons; assumed when the top of the bludgeon or the tip of the edged weapon is pointing upwards.

Handgun - A firearm that can be held and discharged with one hand. Hand Positioning - (See Guard.)

Hang fire - A perceptible delay in the ignition of a cartridge after the primer has been struck.

Head-Hunter - A fighter who primarily attacks the head.

High-Line Kick - One of the two different classifications of a kick. A kick that is directed to targets above an assailant's waist level. (See Low-Line Kick.)

Histrionics - The field of theatrics or acting.

Homicide - The death of another person without legal

justification of excuse.

Hook Kick - A circular kick that can be delivered in both kicking and punching ranges.

Hook Punch - A circular punch that can be delivered in both the punching and grappling ranges.

Hold - A specific manner of grasping or holding an assailant.

Human Shield - Using your assailant's body as a shield or obstacle in combat.

I

Ice Pick Grip - A hand grip used to hold an edged weapon, bludgeon and some makeshift weapons; assumed when the tip of the edged weapon or the top of the bludgeon is pointing downward.

Ice Pick Stick Strangle - A stick strangle used with an ice pick grip.

Immobilization Attack - One of the five conventional methods of attack. A highly complex system of moves and countermoves that allows you to temporarily control and manipulate the assailant's limbs (usually his arms and hands) in order to create an opening of attack.

Impact Power - Destructive force generated by mass and velocity.

Impact Training - A training exercise that develops pain tolerance.

Incapacitate - To disable an assailant by rendering him unconscious or damaging his bones, joints or organs.

Indirect Attack - One of the five conventional methods of attack. A progressive method of attack whereby the initial tool or technique is designed to set the assailant up for follow-up blows.

Initiation Phase - One of the three stages of a stick or bludgeon strike. The initiation phase is initiation point of a swing.

Insertion Points - Specific anatomical targets you can stab with a knife and some makeshift weapons.

Inside Position - The area between both of your assailant's arms where he has the greatest amount of control.

Intent - One of the essential factors to consider when assessing a threatening individual. The assailant's purpose or motive (see Demeanor, Positioning, Range, and Weapon Capability).

Intuition - The innate ability to know or sense something without the use of rational thought.

Intuitive Tool Response (ITR) - Spontaneously reacting with the appropriate combative tool.

J

Jab - A quick, probing punch designed to create openings in the assailant's defense.

Jeet Kune Do - "Way of Intercepting Fist." Bruce Lee's approach to the martial arts, which includes his innovative concepts, theories, methodologies, and philosophies of unarmed combat.

Joint Lock - A grappling range technique that immobilizes the assailant's joint.

Judo - "Gentle Way." A Japanese grappling art (founded by Jigoro Kano in 1882) which is used as a sport. Judo utilizes shoulder and hip throws, foot sweeps, chokes, and pins.

Jujitsu - "Gentleness" or "suppleness." A system of self-defense that is the parent of both Judo and Aikido. Jujitsu specializes in grappling range but is known to employ a few striking techniques.

K

Karate - "Empty hand" or "China hand," a traditional martial art that originated in Okinawa and later spread to Japan and Korea (see Kung-Fu).

Kata - "Pattern" or "Form". A traditional training methodology whereby the practitioner practices a series of prearranged movements.

Kick - 1) A sudden, forceful strike with the foot (see High-Line Kick and Low- Line Kick); 2) The recoil of a firearm.

Kick boxing - A popular combat sport that employs full-contact tools.

Kicking Range - One of the three ranges of unarmed combat. Kicking range is the furthest distance of unarmed combat wherein you use your legs to strike an assailant. (see Grappling Range and Punching Range).

Kicking Range Tools - The various body weapons employed in the kicking range of unarmed combat, including side kicks, push kicks, hook kicks, and vertical kicks.

Killer Instinct - A cold, primal mentality that surges to your consciousness and turns you into a vicious fighter.

Kinesics - The study of nonlinguistic body movement communications (i.e., eye movement, shrugs, facial gestures, etc.).

Kinesiology - The study of principles and mechanics of human movement.

Kinesthetic Perception - The ability to accurately feel your body during the execution of a particular movement.

Kneeling Firearm Stance - A strategic stance you assume when kneeling down with a handgun.

Knife-Defense Stance - One of the many stances used in CFA's system. A strategic stance you assume when face-to-face with an knife or edged weapon attacker. (See De-escalation Stance, Fighting Stance, Knife Fighting Stance, Firearms Stance, Natural Stance, Stick Fighting Stance).

Kung-Fu - "Accomplished task or effort," a term used erroneously to identify the traditional Chinese martial arts (see Karate).

L

Lead Side -The side of the body that faces an assailant.

Leg Block - A blocking technique used with the legs. The leg block can be angled in three different directions: forward, right and left.

Limited Penetration - The (LP) is a corner clearing movement performed by positioning your firearm and one eye around the corner.

Linear Movement - Movements that follow the path of a straight line.

Long Range Combat - The furthest distance of knife and bludgeon combat. At this distance you can only strike or slash your assailant's hand.

Low Maintenance Tool - Offensive and defensive tools that require the least amount of training and practice to maintain proficiency. Low maintenance tools generally don't require preliminary stretching.

Low-Line Kick - One of the two different classifications of a kick. A kick that is directed to targets below the assailant's waist level. (See High-Line Kick.)

Lock - (see Joint Lock).

Loyalty - The state of being faithful to a person, cause, or ideal.

M

Makeshift Weapon - A common everyday object that can be converted into either an offensive or defensive weapon.

There are four Makeshift Weapon classifications in the CFA system: Cutting Makeshift Weapons, Shielding Makeshift Weapons, Distracting Makeshift Weapons, and Striking Makeshift Weapons.

Maneuver - To manipulate into a strategically desired position.

Manipulation Accuracy - The ability to manipulate your assailant's limbs and joints with precision and exactness.

Martial Artist - One who studies and practices the martial arts.

Martial Arts - The traditional "arts of war" (see Karate and Kung-Fu).

Martial Truth - (See Combative Truth.)

Mechanics - (See Body Mechanics.)

Medicine Ball - A large, heavy ball used to strengthen and condition a fighter's stomach muscles.

Meet - A defensive technique that intercepts your assailant's line of attack with a slash.

Mental Attributes - The various cognitive qualities that enhance your fighting skills.

Mental Component - One of the three vital components of the CFA system. The mental component includes the cerebral aspects of fighting including the Killer Instinct, Strategic & Tactical Development, Analysis & Integration, Philosophy and Cognitive Development (see Physical Component and Spiritual Component).

Mesomorph - A body type classified by a high degree of muscularity and strength. (see Endomorph and Ectomorph).

Methods of Attack - The five conventionally recognized methods of attacking. They include: single attack, indirect attack, attack by draw, immobilization attack, and compound attack.

GLOSSARY

Mexican Standoff - A precarious situation where both you and your adversary have the drop on one another.

Mid Phase - One of the three stages of a stick swing. The mid phase is the contact or impact point of the swing.

Mid Range Combat - One of the three ranges of knife and bludgeon combat. At this distance you can strike, slash or stab your assailant's head, arms and body with your weapon.

Misfire - A failure of a cartridge to fire after the primer has been struck.

Mobility - A combative attribute. The ability to move your body quickly and freely while balanced. (see Footwork).

Modern Martial Art - A pragmatic combat art that has evolved to meet the demands and characteristics of the present time.

Modernist - One who subscribes to the philosophy of the modern martial arts.

Modification - To make fundamental changes to serve a new end.

Mounted Position - One of the five general ground fighting positions. The mounted position is where the practitioner sits on top of his assailant's torso or chest.

Mouthpiece - A rubber protector used to cover your teeth when sparring. There are two types of mouthpiece: single and double.

Muscular Endurance - The muscles' ability to perform the same motion or task repeatedly for a prolonged period of time.

Muscular Flexibility - The muscles' ability to move through maximum natural ranges.

Muscular Strength - The maximum force that can be exerted by a particular muscle or muscle group against resistance.

Muscular/Skeletal Conditioning - An element of physical

fitness that entails muscular strength, endurance, and flexibility.

Muzzle - The front end of the barrel.

Muzzle Flash - An incandescent burst of light which is emitted from the muzzle and cylinder of a handgun.

N

Natural Stance - One of the many stances used in CFA's system. A strategic stance you assume when approached by a suspicious person who appears non threatening. (See De-escalation Stance, Fighting Stance, Knife Fighting Stance, Firearms Stance, Knife-Defense Stance, and Stick Fighting Stance).

Neutralize - (See Incapacitate.)

Neutral Zone - The distance outside of the kicking range from which neither the practitioner nor the assailant can touch the other.

Nomenclature Awareness - The ability to understand and recognize the system of names used in combat.

Non aggressive Physiology - Strategic body language used to de-escalate a potentially violent individual.

Non telegraphic Movement - Body mechanics or movements that do not inform an assailant of your intentions.

Nuclear Ground Fighting Tools - Specific grappling range tools designed to inflict immediate and irreversible damage. Some nuclear tools and tactics include: (1) Biting tactics; (2) Tearing tactics; (3) Crushing tactics; (4) Continuous Choking tactics; (5) Gouging techniques; (6) Raking tactics; (7) And all striking techniques.

O

OC (Oleoresin Capsicum, also known as pepper gas) - A natural mixture of oil and cayenne pepper used as a self-defense spray. OC is an inflammatory agent that affects the assailant's mucus membranes (i.e. eyes, nose, throat, lungs).

Offense - The armed and unarmed means and methods of attacking a criminal assailant.

Offensive Flow - A progression of continuous offensive movements or actions designed to neutralize or terminate your adversary. (see Compound Attack).

Offensive Range Manipulation (ORM) - The strategic manipulation of ranges (armed or unarmed) for offensive purposes.

Offensive Reaction Time (ORT) - The elapsed time between target selection and target impaction.

One-Hand Reloading - The process of reloading a firearm with only one hand.

One-Mindedness - A state of deep concentration wherein you are free from all distractions (internal and external).

Opposite Poles - One of the ground fighting positions. The opposite pole position is assumed when both you and your assailant are facing opposite directions. This often occurs when sprawling against your adversary.

Ornamental Techniques - Techniques that are characterized as complex, inefficient, and or impractical for real combat situations.

P

Pain Tolerance - Your ability to physically and psychologically withstand pain. 490

Palming - The strategic concealment of a knife or edged weapon behind the forearm. Also known as Knife Palming.

Panic - The second stage of fear; overpowering fear (see Fright and Terror).

Parry - A defensive technique; a quick, forceful slap that redirects an assailant's linear attack.

ENGAGE WITH RAGE

Pass - A defensive technique used in knife fighting.

Patience - A combative attribute. The ability to endure and tolerate difficulty.

Perception - Interpretation of vital information acquired from your senses when faced with a potentially threatening situation.

Perpendicular Mount - One of the five general ground fighting positions. The perpendicular mount is established when you are lying on top of your adversary and both of your legs are on one side of his body.

Philosophical Resolution - The act of analyzing and answering various questions concerning the use of violence in defense of yourself and others.

Philosophy - One of the five aspects of CFA's mental component. A deep state of introspection whereby you methodically resolve critical questions concerning the use of force in defense of yourself or others.

Physical Attributes - The numerous physical qualities that enhance your combative skills and abilities.

Physical Component - One of the three vital components of the CFA system. The physical component includes the physical aspects of fighting including Physical Fitness, Weapon/Technique Mastery, and Combative Attributes (see Mental Component and Spiritual Component).

Physical Conditioning - (See Combative Fitness).

Pistol - A gun with a short barrel that can be held, aimed, and fired with one hand.

Power - A physical attribute of armed and unarmed combat. The amount of force you can generate when striking an anatomical target.

Physical Fitness - (See Combative Fitness).

Pitch - One of the four components of the human voice. The relative highness or lowness of the voice.

GLOSSARY

Poker Face - A neutral and attentive facial expression that is used when de- escalating a hostile individual. The poker face prevents a hostile person from reading your intentions or feelings.

Positioning - The spatial relationship of the assailant to the assailed person in terms of target exposure, escape, angle of attack, and various other strategic considerations.

Positions of Concealment - Various objects or locations that permit you to temporarily hide from your adversary. Positions of Concealment are most commonly used to evade engagement with your assailant(s) and they permit you to attack with the element of surprise. Positions of Concealment include: trees, shrubbery, behind doors, the dark, walls, stairwells, under cars, large and tall objects, etc.

Positions of Cover - Any object or location that temporarily protects you from the assailant's gun fire. Some Positions of Cover include: large concrete utility poles, large rocks, thick trees, an engine block, corner of a building, concrete steps, etc.

Post Traumatic Syndrome (PTS) - A group of symptoms that may occur in the aftermath of a violent confrontation with a criminal assailant. Common symptoms of Post Traumatic Syndrome include denial, shock, fear, anger, severe depression, sleeping and eating disorders, societal withdrawal, and paranoia.

Power Generator - (See Anatomical Power Generators)

Premise - An axiom, concept, rule or any other valid reason to modify or go beyond that which has been established.

Pressure Point - A point on the body where a nerve lies close to its surface and it is supported by bone or muscle mass.

Probable Reaction Dynamics (PRD) - the opponent's anticipated or predicted movements or actions during both armed and unarmed combat.

Probe - A offensive tool that tests the assailant's combative abilities.

Proficiency Training - A CFA training methodology requiring the practitioner to execute a specific body weapon, technique, maneuver or tactic over and over for a prescribed number or repetitions (see Conditioning Training and Street Training).

Progressive Indirect Attack -(see Indirect Attack).

Proxemics - The study of the nature and effect of man's personal space.

Proximity - The ability to maintain a strategically safe distance from a threatening individual.

Pseudospeciation - A combative attribute. The tendency to assign subhuman and inferior qualities to a threatening assailant.

Psychological Conditioning - The process of conditioning the mind for the horrors and rigors of real combat.

Psycho/Emotional Training - Combative training conducted when you're experiencing different types of emotional states.

Psychomotor Domain - This includes the physical skills and attributes necessary to execute a combative tool, technique or maneuver.

Psychopath - A person with an antisocial personality disorder, especially one manifested in aggressive, perverted, criminal, or amoral behavior.

Pummel - A flurry of full-speed, full-force strikes delivered from the mounted position.

Punch - A quick, forceful strike of the fists.

Punching Range - One of the three ranges of unarmed combat. Punching range is the mid range of unarmed combat from which the fighter uses his hands to strike his assailant. (see Kicking Range and Grappling Range)

Punching Range Tools - The various body weapons that

are employed in the punching range of unarmed combat, including finger jabs, palm heel strikes, rear cross, knife hand strikes, horizontal and shovel hooks, uppercuts, and hammer fist strikes. (see Grappling Range Tools and Kicking Range Tools).

Q

Qualities of Combat - (see Attributes of Combat).

Quick Peek - A technique which is executed from a position of cover by rapidly darting out a small portion of your head and one eye to quickly observe.

R

Range - The spatial relationship between a fighter and a threatening assailant.

Range Deficiency - The inability to effectively fight and defend in all ranges (armed and unarmed) of combat.

Range Manipulation - A combative attribute. The strategic manipulation of combat ranges.

Range Proficiency - A combative attribute. The ability to effectively fight and defend in all ranges (armed and unarmed) of combat.

Ranges of Armed Combat - The various distances a fighter might physically engage with an assailant while involved in armed combat: including knives, bludgeons, projectiles, makeshift weapons, and firearms.)

Ranges of Engagement - (See Combat Ranges).

Ranges of Unarmed Combat - The three distances a fighter might physically engage with an assailant while involved in unarmed combat: kicking range, punching range, and grappling range.

Reaction Dynamics - The assailant's physical response to a particular tool, technique, or weapon after initial contact is made.

Reaction Time - The elapsed time between a stimulus and the response to that particular stimulus (see Offensive Reaction Time and Defensive Reaction Time).

Rear Cross - A straight punch delivered from the rear hand that crosses from right to left (if in a left stance) or left to right (if in a right stance).

Rear Side - The side of the body furthest from the assailant (see Lead Side).

Reasonable Force - That degree of force which is not excessive for a particular event and which is appropriate in protecting yourself or others.

Refinement - The strategic and methodical process of improving or perfecting.

Repetition - Performing a single movement, exercise, strike or action continuously for a specific period.

Research - A scientific investigation or inquiry.

Rest Position - A relaxed posture you assume (when holding a stick or bludgeon) during idle periods in class (i.e., talking to another students, receiving instructions, etc.).

Reverberation Path - The path at which your stick or bludgeon can bounce back at you.

Revolver - A handgun consisting of a cylinder that brings several chambers successively into line with the barrel of the gun.

Rhythm - Movements characterized by the natural ebb and flow of related elements.

Right to Bear Arms - A provision of the Second Amendment to the United States Constitution that prohibits our government from interfering with the right of the people to arm themselves.

Rimfire - A firearm cartridge which has its primer located around the rim of the case bottom.

Round - 1) A period of time. 2) A single unit of ammunition (see Cartridge).

S

Safe Room - A strategic location in your residence where you and family members can escape from an intruder who has entered your home.

Safety - One of the three criteria for a CFA body weapon, technique, maneuver or tactic. It means the that the tool, technique, maneuver or tactic provides the least amount of danger and risk for the practitioner (see Efficiency and Effectiveness).

Scissors Hold - (see Guard).

Secondary Hand - A close quarter technique used in both knife and bludgeon fighting whereby you temporarily hold your assailant's weapon hand in place after you have employed a defensive maneuver.

Secondary Weapons - Various natural body weapons that are applied during armed combat.

Selective Semantics - The selection and utilization of strategic words to de-escalate a hostile person. Also known as Choice Words.

Self-Awareness - One of the three categories of CFA awareness. Knowing and understanding yourself. This includes aspects of yourself which may provoke criminal violence and which will promote a proper and strong reaction to an attack. (see Criminal Awareness and Situational Awareness.)

Self-Confidence - Having trust and faith in yourself.

Self-Defense - The act of defending yourself or one's family (also called Personal Protection or Self-Protection).

Self-Enlightenment - The state of knowing your capabilities, limitations, character traits, feelings, general attributes, and motivations (see Self- Awareness.)

    Semiautomatic Handgun - (see Autoloader).

    Sensei - Teacher.

    Set - A term used to describe a grouping of repetitions.

    Setup Tool - A tool used to throw the assailant off balance and/or open his defenses.

    Shadow Fighting - A CFA training exercise used to develop and refine your tools, techniques, and attributes of armed and unarmed combat.

    Shielding Makeshift Weapon - One of the four types of CFA makeshift weapons. Any object that can be used to effectively shield oneself from an assailant's attack (see also Distracting Makeshift Weapon, Cutting Makeshift Weapon, and Striking Makeshift Weapon.)

    Shooting Accuracy - The ability to shoot a firearm with precision and exactness.

    Shot - A package or wad of metal balls that vary in size and spread out as they travel away from the muzzle of a shot gun.

    Shotgun - A single-or double-barreled, smooth-bore firearm used for firing shot or slugs at a relatively close distance.

    Shoulder Roll - A defensive technique that rocks your body away from a punch in order to nullify its force.

    Side Fall - A firearm engagement technique which is executed from a kneeling position behind cover.

    Sifu - (See Sensei.)

    Sight Alignment - A component of marksmanship whereby you correctly align your dominant eye with both the front and rear sights of your firearm.

    Sights - Various electronic, optical, and mechanical devices used to aim a firearm.

    Single Action - A type of pistol action in which pulling the trigger will release the hammer.

GLOSSARY

Single Attack - One of the five conventional methods of attack. A method of attack whereby you deliver a solitary offensive strike. It may involve a series of discreet probes or one swift, powerful strike aimed at terminating the encounter. (See Compound Attack, Indirect Attack, Immobilization Attack, and Attack By Draw).

Situational Awareness - One of the three categories of CFA awareness. A state of being totally alert to your immediate surroundings, including people, places, objects, and actions. (see Criminal Awareness and Self-Awareness.)

Skeletal Alignment - The proper alignment or arrangement of your body. Skeletal Alignment maximizes the structural integrity of striking tools.

Slash - One of the two ways to cut someone with a knife or edged weapon. A quick, sweeping stroke of a knife (see Stab.)

Slipping - A defensive maneuver that permits you to avoid an assailant's linear blow without stepping out of range. Slipping can be accomplished by quickly snapping the head and upper torso sideways (right or left) to avoid the blow.

Snap Back - A defensive maneuver that permits you to avoid an assailant's linear and circular blow without stepping out of range. The snap back can be accomplished by quickly snapping the head backwards to avoid the assailant's blow.

Somatotyping - A method of classifying human body types or builds into three different categories: ectomorph, mesomorph, and endomorph.

Speed - A physical attribute of armed and unarmed combat. The rate or a measure of the rapid rate of motion.

Spinning Kicks - Kicks delivered with a spin of the body.

Spinning Punches - Punches delivered with a spin of the body.

Spiritual Component - One of the three vital components of the CFA system. The spiritual component includes the metaphysical issues and aspects of existence (see Physical Component and Mental Component).

Sprawling - A defensive technique in grappling range. The sprawl technique is accomplished by lowering your hips to the ground while simultaneously shooting both of your legs back.

Square-Off - To be face-to-face with a hostile or threatening assailant who is about to attack you.

Squib Load - A cartridge which develops less than normal velocity after the ignition of a cartridge.

Stab - One of the two ways to cut someone with a knife or edged weapon. A quick thrust made with a pointed weapon or implement, usually a knife. (see Slash.)

Stable Terrain - Terrain which is principally characterized as stationary, compact, dense, hard, flat, dry, or solid.

Stance - One of the many strategic postures that you assume prior to or during armed or unarmed combat.

Stance Selection - A combative attribute. The ability to instinctively select a stance appropriate for a particular combat situation.

Standing Firearm Stance - A strategic stance you assume when standing with a handgun.

Step and Drag - Strategic footwork used when standing on unstable terrain. Stick Block - A defensive technique that stops your assailant's stick strike.

Stick Deflection - A defensive technique that deflects and redirects your assailant's stick strike.

Stick Twirl - A dexterity exercise performed with either one or two sticks. Stop-Hit - A method of hitting the assailant before his tool reaches full extension.

Stopping Power - A firearm's ability to stop the assailant from continuing any further action.

Strategic Leaning - A defensive maneuver which permits

GLOSSARY

you to evade a knife slash while remaining in range to counter.

Strategic Positioning - Tactically positioning yourself to either escape, move behind a barrier, or use a makeshift weapon.

Strategy - A carefully planned method of achieving your goal of engaging an assailant under advantageous conditions.

Street Fight - A spontaneous and violent confrontation between two or more individuals wherein no rules apply.

Street Fighter - An unorthodox combatant who has no formal training. His combative skills and tactics are usually developed in the street by the process of trial and error.

Street Smarts - Having the knowledge, skills and attitude necessary to avoid, defuse, confront, and neutralize both armed and unarmed assailants.

Street Training - A CFA training methodology requiring the practitioner to deliver explosive compound attacks for ten to twenty seconds (see Conditioning Training and Proficiency Training).

Strength Training - The process of developing muscular strength through systematic application of progressive resistance.

Striking Accuracy - The ability to strike your assailant with precision and exactness (this includes natural body weapons, bludgeons and some makeshift weapons).

Striking Art - A combat art that relies predominantly on striking techniques to neutralize or terminate a criminal attacker.

Striking Tool - 1) A natural body weapon that impacts with the assailant's anatomical target. 2) A hand-held implement that impacts with the assailant's anatomical target.

Striking Makeshift Weapon - One of the four types of CFA makeshift weapons. Any object that can be used to effectively strike a criminal assailant (see also Distracting Makeshift

Weapon, Cutting Makeshift Weapon, and Shielding Makeshift Weapon.)

Strong Side - The strongest and most coordinated side of your body. Structure - A definite and organized pattern.

Style - The distinct manner in which a fighter executes or performs his combat skills.

Stylistic Integration - The purposeful and scientific collection of tools and techniques from various disciplines, which are strategically integrated and dramatically altered to meet three essential criteria: efficiency, effectiveness, and combative safety.

System - The unification of principles, philosophies, rules, strategies, methodologies, tools, and techniques or a particular method of combat.

T

Tactical Calming - (See De-Escalation.)

Tactic - The skill of using the available means to achieve an end.

Tactical Option Selection - A combative attribute. The ability to select the appropriate tactical option for any particular self-defense situation.

Tactile Sight - A combative attribute. The ability to "see" through tactile contact with your assailant.

Takedowns - Various grappling maneuvers designed to take your assailant down to the ground.

Target Exploitation - A combative attribute. The strategic maximization of your assailant's reaction dynamics during a fight. Target Exploitation can be applied in both armed and unarmed encounters.

Target Impaction - The successful striking of the appropriate anatomical target.

Target Orientation - A combative attribute. Having a

workable knowledge of the assailant's anatomical targets. Target orientation is divided into five different categories: (1) Impact Targets - anatomical targets that can be struck with your natural body weapons; (2) Non-Impact Targets - anatomical targets that can be strangled, twisted, torn, crushed, clawed, gouged, broken, dislocated, or strategically manipulated; (3) Edged Weapon Targets - anatomical targets that can be punctured or slashed with a knife or edged weapon; (4) Bludgeon Targets - anatomical targets that can be struck with a stick or bludgeon; (5) Ballistic Targets - anatomical targets that can be shot by a firearm.

Target Recognition - The ability to immediately recognize appropriate anatomical targets during an emergency self-defense situation.

Target Selection - The process of mentally selecting the appropriate anatomical target for your self-defense situation. This is predicated on certain factors, including proper force response, assailant's positioning and range.

Target Stare - A form of telegraphing whereby you stare at the anatomical target you intend to strike.

Target Zones - The three areas which an assailant's anatomical targets are located. (See Zone One, Zone Two and Zone Three.)

Technique - A systematic procedure by which a task is accomplished.

Telegraphic Cognizance - A combative attribute. The ability to recognize both verbal and non-verbal signs of aggression or assault.

Telegraphing - Unintentionally making your intentions known to your adversary. Tempo - The speed or rate at which you speak.

Terrain - The type of surface that you are standing on. There are two classifications of terrain: stable and unstable. (See Stable Terrain and Unstable Terrain)

Terrain Orientation - A combative attribute. Having a working knowledge of the various types of environmental terrains and their advantages, dangers, and strategic limitations.

Terror - The third stage of fear; defined as overpowering fear (see Fright and Panic).

Throw - Grappling techniques designed to unbalance your assailant and lift him off the floor.

Timing - A physical and mental attribute or armed and unarmed combat. Your ability to execute a movement at the optimum moment.

Tone - The overall quality or character of your voice.

Tool - (See Body Weapon.)

Traditional Style/System - (See Traditional Martial Art.)

Traditionalism - The beliefs and principles of a traditional or classical martial art.

Traditionalist - One who subscribes to the principles and practices of traditional martial arts.

Traditional Martial Arts - Any martial art that fails to evolve and meet the demands and characteristics of the present time (see Karate and Kung-Fu).

Training Drills - The various exercises and drills aimed at perfecting combat skills, attributes, and tactics.

Training Methodologies - Training procedures utilized in the CFA system.

Training Zone - The training zone (or target heart rate) is a safe and effective level of physical activity that produces cardiorespiratory fitness.

Trapping - Momentarily immobilizing or manipulating the assailant's limb or limbs in order to create an opening to attack.

Trapping Range - The distance between punching and

grappling range in which trapping techniques are attempted.

Traversing Skills - Pivoting and twisting laterally. Traversing skills can be used for both armed and unarmed combat.

Trigger Squeeze - A component of marksmanship. Trigger Squeeze is achieved by squeezing the trigger of your firearm straight to the rear in a smooth and fluid manner without disturbing the sight alignment.

Trouble Shooting Skills - A combative attribute. The ability to immediately diagnose and solve problems when engaged with the adversary.

U

Unified Mind - A mind which is free and clear of distractions and focused on the combative situation.

Uniform Crime Report (UCR) - A nationwide cooperative statistical compilation of the efforts and reports of 16,000 state and local law enforcement agencies that voluntarily report data on crime.

Unstable Terrain - Terrain which is characterized as mobile, uneven, flexible, slippery, wet, or rocky. (See Stable Terrain).

Unstructured Modernist - A martial artist who adheres to the abstract principles of combative formlessness.

Use of Force Response - A combative attribute. Selecting the appropriate level of force for a particular emergency self-defense situation.

V

V-Grip - A strategically defensive grip used to defend against an edged weapon attack.

Vertical Trapping - Trapping techniques that are applied while standing face to face with your adversary. (See Immobilization Attack).

Viciousness - A combative attribute. Dangerously

aggressive behavior. Victim - Any person who is the object of a particular crime.

Visualization - The purposeful formation of mental images and scenarios in the mind's eye.

Visual Monitoring Points - Specific points or locations on your assailant that you should look at during an emergency self-defense situation.

W

Warm-up - A series of mild exercises, stretches, and movement designed to prepare you for more intense exercise.

Weak Side - The weakest and most uncoordinated side of your body.

Weapon and Technique Mastery - A component of CFA's physical component. The kinesthetic and psychomotor development of a weapon or combative technique.

Weapon Capability - An assailant's ability to use and attack with a particular weapon.

Weapon Hierarchy Mastery - Possessing the knowledge, skills and attitude necessary to master the complete hierarchy of combat weapons.

Weapon Uniformity - Gripping and/or drawing your hand-held weapon the same way every time.

Webbing - The first phase of the Widow Maker Program. Webbing is a two hand strike delivered to the assailant's chin. It is called Webbing because your hands resemble a large web that wraps around the enemy's face.

Western Boxing - A Western combat sport that only employs punching-range tools.

Widow Maker Program – A CFA program specifically designed to teach the law abiding citizen how to use extreme force when faced with immediate threat of unlawful deadly criminal attack. The Widow Maker program is divided into two phases or methodologies: Webbing and Razing.

Y

Yell - A loud and aggressive scream or shout used for various strategic reasons.

Z

Zero Beat – One of the four beat classifications of the Widow Maker, Feral Fighting and Savage Street Fighting Programs. Zero beat strikes are full pressure techniques applied to a specific target until ruptures. They include gouging, crushing, biting, and choking techniques.

Zone One - Anatomical targets related to your senses, including the eyes, temple, nose, chin, and back of neck.

Zone Three - Anatomical targets related to your mobility, including thighs, knees, shins, and instep.

Zone Two - Anatomical targets related to your breathing, including front of neck, solar plexus, ribs, and groin.

Zoning - A defensive maneuver designed to negate your assailant's stick strike through strategic movement and precise timing. Zoning can be accomplished by either moving into the direction of your assailant's strike (before it generates significant force) or by moving completely out of his stick's arc.

ENGAGE WITH RAGE

Suggested Reading & Viewing

SUGGESTED READING (BOOKS):

• Boxing Domination: A 21-Day Program to Psych-Out, Confuse, Frustrate, and Beat Your Opponent in Boxing and MMA

• Power Boxing Workout Secrets

• Speed Boxing Secrets: A 21-Day Program to Hitting Faster and Reacting Quicker in Boxing and Martial Arts

• Knife Fighting: A Step-by-Step Guide to Practical Knife Fighting for Self-Defense

• The 10 Best Knife Fighting Techniques

• The 10 Best Power Punches: For Boxing, Martial Arts, MMA and Self-Defense

• The 10 Best Mental Toughness Exercises

• The 10 Best Ways to Defeat Multiple Attackers

• The 10 Best Ways to Develop Your Killer Instinct:

• The 10 Best Bar Fighting Moves: Down and Dirty Fighting Techniques to Save Your Ass When Things Get Ugly

• The 10 Best Sucker Punch Tricks

• Survival Weapons: A User's Guide to the Best Self-Defense Weapons for Any Dangerous Situation

• Knockout: The Ultimate Guide to Sucker Punching

• The 10 Best Kicking Techniques

• The 10 Best Stick Fighting Techniques

• Cane Fighting: The Authoritative Guide to Using the Cane or Walking Stick for Self-Defense

• The Heavy Bag Bible: 3 Best-Selling Heavy Bag Books In One Massive Collection

• Double End Bag Workout

• The 10 Best Things To Do When Held At Gunpoint

• The 10 Best Ways To Defeat Multiple Attackers

• The 10 Best Things To Do During a Mass Shooting

ENGAGE WITH RAGE

- The 10 Best Stick Fighting Techniques
- Bruce Lee's 5 Methods of Attack
- The Widow Maker Compendium (Books 1-3)
- Heavy Bag Workout
- Heavy Bag Combinations
- Invincible: Mental Toughness Techniques for the Street, Battlefield and Playing Field
- Unleash Hell
- Feral Fighting
- Savage Street Fighting
- Stand and Deliver
- The Widow Maker Program
- Maximum Damage
- Kubotan Power
- The Complete Body Opponent Bag Book
- Self-Defense Tips & Tricks
- Heavy Bag Training: Boxing, Mixed Martial Arts & Self-Defense
- Out of the Cage: A Complete Guide to Beating a Mixed Martial Artist on the Street
- Gun Safety: For Home Defense and Concealed Carry
- Warrior Wisdom: Inspiring Ideas from the World's Greatest Warriors
- Ground War: How to Destroy a Grappler in a Street Fight
- War Craft: Street Fighting Tactics of the War Machine
- War Machine: How to Transform Yourself into a Vicious and Deadly Street Fighter
- The Bigger They Are, The Harder They Fall: How to Defeat a Larger & Stronger Adversary in a Street Fight
- First Strike: Mastering the Preemptive Strike for Street Combat
- When Seconds Count: Everyone Guide to Self Defense
- Killer Instinct: Unarmed Combat for Street Survival
- Street Lethal: Unarmed Urban Combat

SUGGESTED READING & VIEWING

SUGGESTED VIEWING (VIDEOS):

- Combat Energy Drills
- Punching Mitts: Drills & Workout Routines
- Judge, Jury & Executioner
- Pepper Spray: A Video Guide to Using Pepper Spray for Self Defense
- Pressure Points: The Science of Striking Vital Targets
- Sparring: Tips: Tips, Tactics & Techniques to Dominate Your Opponent
- Kubotans & Yawaras: A Quick & Dirty Guide
- Submission Fighting for the Street (Volume 1)
- Submission Fighting for the Street (Volume 2)
- Submission Fighting for the Street (Volume 3)
- Medicine Ball Workout (Volume 1)
- Medicine Ball Workout (Volume 2)
- Double End Bag Training
- Heavy Bag Training
- Power Punching
- Speed Training for Street Fighting (Volume 1): Visual Reflexes
- Speed Training for Street Fighting (Volume 2): Tactile Reflexes
- Speed Training for Street Fighting (Volume 3): Recognition & Auditory Reflexes
- Speed Training for Street Fighting (Volume 4): Movement Speed
- Wrist Locks For The Street (Volume 1)
- Wrist Locks For The Street (Volume 2)
- Choke Out
- Body Opponent Bag Training
- War Machine II
- Sneak Peek
- Armed to the Teeth (Volume 1)
- Armed to the Teeth (Volume 2)

ENGAGE WITH RAGE

- Defend or Die
- Escape Master
- In Your Face
- Engage With Rage
- First Strike
- Ground Fighting in The Streets
- Batter Up
- Under The Gun
- Street Stick Fighting
- Use It or Lose It
- Rat Packed
- ,Ground Pounders
- Control & Conquer (Volume 1)
- Control & Conquer (Volume 2)
- Savage Street Fighting: Tactical Savagery As A Last Resort
- The WidowMaker Program: Maximum Punishment for Extreme Situations
- Feral Fighting Program: Level 2 WidowMaker
- War Blade Program: A Complete Guide to Tactical Knife Fighting

About Sammy Franco

With over 35 years of experience, Sammy Franco is one of the world's foremost authorities on armed and unarmed self-defense. Highly regarded as a leading innovator in combat sciences, Mr. Franco was one of the premier pioneers in the field of "reality-based" self-defense and martial arts instruction.

Sammy Franco is perhaps best known as the founder and creator of Contemporary Fighting Arts (CFA), a state-of-the-art offensive- based combat system that is specifically designed for real-world self-defense. CFA is a sophisticated and practical system of self-defense, designed specifically to provide efficient and effective methods to avoid, defuse, confront, and neutralize both armed and unarmed attackers.

Sammy Franco has frequently been featured in martial art magazines, newspapers, and appeared on numerous radio and television programs. Mr. Franco has also authored numerous books, magazine articles, and editorials, and has developed a popular library of instructional videos.

Sammy Franco's experience and credibility in the combat sciences is unequaled. One of his many accomplishments in this field includes the fact that he has earned the ranking of a Law Enforcement Master Instructor, and has designed, implemented, and taught officer survival training to the United States Border Patrol (USBP). He has instructed members of the US Secret Service, Military Special Forces, Washington DC Police Department, Montgomery County, Maryland Deputy Sheriffs, and the US Library of Congress Police. Sammy Franco is also a member of the prestigious International Law

Enforcement Educators and Trainers Association (ILEETA) as well as the American Society of Law Enforcement Trainers (ASLET) and he is listed in the "Who's Who Director of Law Enforcement Instructors."

Sammy Franco is a nationally certified Law Enforcement Instructor in the following curricula: PR-24 Side-Handle Baton, Police Arrest and Control Procedures, Police Personal Weapons Tactics, Police Power Handcuffing Methods, Police Oleoresin Capsicum Aerosol Training (OCAT), Police Weapon Retention and Disarming Methods, Police Edged Weapon Countermeasures and "Use of Force" Assessment and Response Methods.

Mr. Franco holds a Bachelor of Arts degree in Criminal Justice from the University of Maryland. He is a regularly featured speaker at a number of professional conferences and conducts dynamic and enlightening seminars on numerous aspects of self-defense and combat training.

On a personal level, Sammy Franco is an animal lover, who will go to great lengths to assist and rescue animals. Throughout the years, he's rescued everything from turkey vultures to goats. However, his most treasured moments are always spent with his beloved German Shepherd dogs.

For more information about Mr. Franco, you can visit his website at: ContemporaryFightingArts.com

www.ingramcontent.com/pod-product-compliance
Lightning Source LLC
Chambersburg PA
CBHW071654090426
42738CB00009B/1525